BOO!!

GHOSTS I HAVE(N'T) LOVED.

To Fred & Debbie
May you have
Health
Wealth
Happiness
in abundance
Sincerely
Najla

AS ENCOUNTERED BY

NAJLA MADY

Dedication

Dedicated in loving and lasting memory
of my Father Abdul Satar Mady

Table of Contents

Canadian Cataloguing in Publication Data

Mady, Najla. 1938-
    BOO!! Ghosts I Have(n't) Loved

ISBN 1-55021-089-0

1. Exorcism – Ontario – Niagara Peninsula.
2. Ghosts – Ontario – Niagara Peninsula.   I. Title

BF1559.M33   1993   133.4'27'0971338   C93–095245–6

Front cover illustration by Trevor Keen, Toronto.
Front cover design by Trevor Keen and Judith Gauthier, Toronto.
Book design and typesetting by Steven Hain, Toronto.
This book was typeset and assembled using an Apple Macintosh Quadra 840AV and Quark Xpress 3.11. The typefaces employed are Candida and Peignot. The front cover illustration was created in Adobe Photoshop 2.0

We would like to thank the Ontario Arts Council, the Ontario Publishing Centre, the Ontario Ministry of Culture, Tourism and Recreation, the Canada Council and the Government of Canada, Department of Communications for their assistance in the production of this book.

New Canada Publications, a division of NC Press Limited,
Box 452, Station A, Toronto, Ontario, Canada, M5W 1H8

Printed and bound in Canada.

PREFACE

It is that time of year again,

*"When yellow leaves, or none, or few, do hang
upon those boughs which shake against the cold."*

Halloween is the festival of *fire* and *dead*, and the *powers of darkness*, which marks the transition from Autumn to Winter, when shivering hungry ghosts from the bare fields and leafless woodland seek shelter in the cottages by the familiar fireside. It is the season of bonfires on hills, fortune telling, offerings of food and drink put out for the spirits, of blood curdling masks, grotesque costumes to keep the evil away, while demons and hobgoblins and witches straddle broomsticks and shankbones in the night sky, and there is the fireside chatter of ghost stories. Najla Mady's book chimes with the season. I am sure the readers will relish every stitch of this collection and enjoy them, for

*Deep night, dark night, the silence of the night,
The time when screech owls cry, and barn dogs howl,
And spirits walk, and ghosts break up their graves,
That time best fits the work we have in hand.*

Under the aura of Romanticism we are perpetually fascinated by their fears. What is hidden under the surface of life, the other side of the coin, is the shadow of the shadow. Secretly the human psyche wishes to explore it and often awaits the witching hour. It is in this feeling of fear that the Romantic mind discovers its creative impulse.

Throughout the Middle Ages the supernatural dominated both literature and life. Those were the times of the sabbat and the witch. Ancient chronicles reveal horrible incidents and facts more sinister than any writer of fiction could conceive. There were learned treatises of ghosts and apparitions.

History records that Padmasambhava, the far-famed professor of occult sciences at the great Buddhist University of Nalanda, was summoned to Lhasa in 747 A.D. by the Emperor of Tibet to exorcise a demoniacal and malignant spirit. Once a disciple of Buddha, Pindola by name and an expert in the occult sciences who had transgressed the Master's will and thus been deprived of nirvana, or salvation, was expelled by the monastic administration to wander disconsolate. He was punished for having brought the dead back to life.

Today, Ed and Lorraine Warren of Connecticut are world experts in psychic phenomena and great seekers of the supernatural, whose clairvoyant powers are amazing and bloodcurdling. Their intensive research on over 3,500 cases of reported phenomena has convinced them beyond a shadow of doubt of the existence of ghosts, demons, witches and vampires. Professor Paul Karan of Kentucky tells me he has spent a night with the ghost of Sherpa Prem Shamsher in a ruined cottage in the remote Himalayan valley. So there are more things in Heaven and Earth that we can never dream of.

In the dim corridors of the Haunted House prowl the ghosts of such literary craftsmen who experimented with aesthetic supernatural themes and fostered the genre of macabre tales. This spectral show first reveals the bearded face of Joseph Sheridan Le Fanu whose artistic tales continue to haunt us. Next to him, in the fading twilight, we discern the bespectacled face of M.R. James, the master creator of the antiquarian ghost story. In the muffled darkness beyond stands the figure of Algernon Blackwood, the modern conjuror of "cosmic" apparitions, followed by several exponents of the ghostly saga like Arthur Machen, E.F. Benson, Oliver Onions and Walter De La Mare. Then there are many more shadowy figures unrecognized in the gathering gothic gloom.

Ghosts have stalked this earth since the early ages, while collected tales of the supernatural and anthologies of ghost stories have always been popular by providing shudder and delight. *The Supernatural Omnibus* by Montague Summers and *The London Mystery Magazine* have created a further craze for thrilling encounters with the world of phantoms— even in the twentieth century! Today we have *The Oxford Book of English Ghost Stories* and *Victorian Ghost Stories*, both jointly edited by Michael Cox and R.A. Gilbert; *The Great American Ghost Stories* by McSherry, Waugh and Greenburg; *The Oxford Book of Canadian Ghost Stories* by Alberto Manguel; *The Penguin Book of Ghost Stories*; and finally *The Mammoth Book of Ghost Stories* by Richard Dalby completes the important listing. Other revivalists and editors in Britain have been Peter Haining and Denis Whitley. There is even a flourishing Ghost Story Society in England.

Najla Mady is a noted clairvoyant and expert of the phenomena of the beyond—the twilight world of psychic fancy wherein she has probed deeper into the surface of things. She has endeavoured to collect a number of ghost stories from the environs of Niagara-on-the-Lake and the wide stretches of Ontario and elsewhere.

The tales she offers do not radiate from any rainbow world of fantasy. The reader is to be reminded that these entertaining ghost stories are indeed true events. They are not the figment of someone's imagination but the product of a professional psychic counsellor's work in the real world.

Although Najla Mady communes with spirits and deals in the supernatural, she approaches her psychic work in a business-like fashion that is based on common sense. She walks among us an ordinary mortal, "not terribly impressed" with her psychic ability. Yet, who can say that she herself is not an angel in our midst?

The best way of relishing a ghost story is to believe in ghosts. One is reminded of the witty remark of truthful Madame du Deffand who, when asked "Do you believe in ghosts?" replied: "No, but I am afraid of them!"

Devendra P. Varma
September, 1993

Introduction

The stories I've compiled and written for this book are true accounts of ghostly and supernatural situations in which I've been directly involved. I don't hunt ghosts nor do I investigate the paranormal, I leave that to others. The paranormal is my normal life. It finds me in my daily work as a professional psychic. My clients bring their ghostly suspicions to me and seek my help in dealing with unnatural intrusions in their lives.

I deal with each situation in the same manner. I begin by explaining that a ghost is nothing more than a restless soul looking for peace and needing a little guidance in finding it. I'll then describe to my client as we sit in my office (or over the phone if they've contacted me in this manner), disturbances that they've seen or felt. This would include noises, smells, feelings, cold air currents, electrical equipment and appliances, or lights turning themselves on and off. Even apparitions!

These descriptions seem to amaze everyone, yet I don't see any difference between being able to pick up information during a personal psychic reading or in this manner. I don't need a person in front of me to pick up information psychically for them. I've spoken with thousands of callers on live radio and television shows over the years and just as a ghost is out there somewhere, so are the callers' voices which I respond to over phone lines with electronic equipment.

Being psychic is the ability to work in the abstract, which includes people. It's all the same to me. To put a spirit to rest

I have to be at the location of the disturbing occurrences. I have to face the subject I'll be dealing with. I ask those who have been involved in a sighting, or who have felt a spirit's presence, to be with me when I meet the ghost. No others are allowed, including friends, relatives, neighbours or media. I refuse to allow my work to be performed in a circus-like atmosphere.

There is yet another reason for this objection. A spirit can travel; they've been known to fly into the body of a bystander in search of a home. Some spirits are defiantly stubborn and preferring to cling to the earth plane, will latch on to any physical body present. This would become a possession, which is to be avoided at all costs.

These simple precautions are a necessary safety measure. I've never had a problem securing an agreement from a client because I've worked with the public for so many years, and my thoughts on the subject are well known. Clients are also aware that I'll take no form of payment to rid their homes of unwanted ghostly guests. I feel my ability is for the benefit of others. My payment is the satisfaction I receive that peace will be restored to a once troubled family because of this ability. I feel fortunate and blessed to possess this attribute. Accepting it was a gradual process, however. I was thirty-eight years of age before I went public waiting thirty-four years before I 'came out.'

Each case I work on is unique. However, my technique never varies. I only have to face the entity and will it to its rest and peace. Unequivocally it does, ordinarily in less than thirty minutes.

Abnormal? Definitely not! A ghost is dead. Death is a normal extension of life. Instead of dealing with death, I'm dealing with life. Frightening? No, there's nothing to fear but fear itself. Know these words, study them, use them, embrace them and you'll feel equal to life.

The true stories on the following pages will introduce

you to various types of ghosts. Since death neither diminish-
es nor changes the personality, I'm forced to deal with varied
ghostly personalities and encounters.

I use terms throughout this book that are best understood
by the general public. Normally I'd not use the word ghost
in conversation, I prefer spirit. Ghost, however, is the most
commonly used word associated with hauntings. Hauntings
or haunted are also words I don't use. I prefer to use 'disturbances.' This publication is to allow the reader to better
understand para- psychology. I've used colloquial terms.

The changing of the personality happens only after the
soul, or spirit, has 'crossed over' into the state of Bardo. It
accepts its death state and moves on to spiritually develop
its soul in preparation for re-birth.

This leads us into the topic of reincarnation.

The material in this publication deals with ghosts—enti-
ties not yet willing to cross over. A complete discussion of
reincarnation is best left for another time.

I've chosen to share two accounts of what is commonly
called Black Magic. An act heinous in itself, but when perpetrated by the victim's own mother, becomes almost
unspeakable.

Each case is a study into the abnormal personality profil-
ing jealousy, envy, hate, insecurity and the pathological
need to control—the enemies of love, understanding and
compassion. It is truly difficult to comprehend why a mother
would choose to wish harm on her child, but it does happen.
For that reason it begs to be discussed.

Knowledge is an enemy of evil and should be embraced
as a gift instead of feared. For those reasons I've held nothing back. There are no details omitted. I'm aware in each
case that feelings of revulsion may surface in the reader. We
need to focus our thoughts on the result, instead of the dis-
tressing situations. The results are satisfactory in each
instance. Let's all live in peace with that knowledge.

From the bizarre, we move into benign types of ghosts. I deal with a varied array of personalities; a son, a grandson, a friend, an assistant cook/waitress and a widow whose husband visited me by walking through a screen door. Normal instances without any outstanding occurrences. These contrasts need to be mentioned as well as the more bizarre. Several chapters are about ghosts I have loved. Being transported back in history is a thrill afforded to a very few. I do, therefore, feel especially fortunate to have 'met' Captain Swayze of the Angel Inn, Niagara-on-the-Lake, Ontario and Frank Hawley's ghostly house guests.

ABOUT NAJLA

"Although we each have an ability to respond to psychic phenomena, you cannot study how to be psychic. You cannot even develop it. You are either psychic or not."

Najla Mady,
Simply Psychic

Born in Quebec, Najla Mady was aware she had psychic abilities as soon as she could speak. Her parents did not discourage her from using her special gifts, and she shared with them incidents of her psychic knowledge as early as the age of four. One day in school, when she was eight, she announced the death of her father to her teacher, then immediately left for home to say farewell to the father she so adored.

At the age of 38, Najla went public. She became a regular favorite guest on television and radio programmes. A popular guest on television programmes such as CBC's Barbara McLeod Show, Najla has been much courted by the media.

However, with her television début came mixed feelings about media exposure, since Najla abhors sensationalism and public display. She decided to continue, since she saw in it the opportunity to educate people in the field of psychic phenomena, to give the public a standard for comparison and to help bring to light those unscrupulous charlatans who played on peoples' emotions and gullibility.

Within two years, she was doing her own weekly media shows: *The Najla Mady Show*, a two-hour radio show on CKTB and *A Psychic Hour with Najla*, a call-in TV show that showcased her ability to do spontaneous psychic readings at a distance. In *A Psychic Hour with Najla*, she predicted the assassination of Anwar Sadat the day before it occured. Among the many, many accurate predictions on world events, scientific discoveries and medical break-throughs made over television: the safe landing of the spy satellite Cosmos 1402 on January 24, 1984, between the Indian Ocean and the Arabian Sea; several tragic airplane crashes; war events in Israel and other countries; and the great archeological discovery of a huge underground river in Alberta.

Accurate and matter-of-fact communications are her trade mark.... *No dippy, chanting, star-gazing fanatic, this woman.* Najla Mady conducts her psychic business with common-sense and professionalism. Ever pragmatic, she has been a pro-active player in community affairs and politics.

When she was writing her first book, *Simply Psychic*, Najla was active on the Executive Board of Directors of a local business club and on the Mayor's Steering Committee Against Drunk Drivers. She attended conferences chaired by then-Premier Bill Davis and Attorney General Roy McMurtey and participated in numerous legislative workshops giving rise to the adoption of new laws in Canada.

Najla has been an active participant in the municipal, provincial and federal political arenas. She has been a member of the Provincial Council and the Governing Body of a major political party; she has made presentations, participated in debates, and helped draft resolutions and policy papers.

Political activist and clairvoyant, straight-shooting yet tender and fun-loving in her personal relationships, Najla is a multi-faceted and terrifically gifted woman. She does psychic readings for people from all walks of life, all over the world, chatting nonchalently with sheiks, priests, doctors, politicians, businessmen and historians. When she is not doing personal counselling or finding lost people and lost articles, she exorcizes ghosts from homes and other places. This book contains only a few of the many ghostly experiences in Najla's life, which she takes in casual stride.

People's reaction to Najla's exorcisms, predictions and pronouncements are that of surprise, amazement, stupefaction and awe. While little concerned about her special powers, Najla is very concerned about helping and educating people. She explains her attitude to her profession in the field of parapsychology thus:

> *"The years have shown me that the subject matter is grossly misunderstood, often held in awe...and has been at times terribly overrated."*

> *"...it takes self-discipline, and responsible application...the talent just is. I don't worry about it, nor am I terribly impressed by it either."*

Although her psychic abilities have thrust her into the media limelight and inspired numerous articles in newspapers and magazines, she seeks neither fame nor fortune, only to help others. In her previous book, *Simply Psychic* (accepted into the Edgar Cayce Foundation library), Najla names the real reward for her often-unremunerated work: *"The benefits...are enormous.... People, beautiful people.... There are no words adequate enough to express the feelings I have for the thousands of people who have passed through my life.... I treasure every one and count myself among one of life's fortunate for having been blessed with the opportunity to be a part of their lives..."*

CHAPTER 1

IN HIS MOTHER'S HOUSE

I had just finished a psychic reading when my client made an inquiry about some family friends. The husband's mother had recently died, and she asked me how their marriage would fare. My response was immediate. "She's not dead! She's very much alive and disturbing them just as she did in life. Her spirit is living in their home, as determined to destroy her son's marriage in death as she was in life."

"Is that right? What can be done?" my alarmed client asked. "The spirit must be put to rest by someone experienced in such matters," was my reply.

The family had immigrated to Canada from the Mediterranean and were of the Orthodox faith. I suggested that they contact their priest. I explained to the concerned friend the service of exorcism used in such instances.

I gave the incident no further thought until several years later when the daughter-in-law of the dead woman came to me for a psychic reading. She introduced herself to me as

Angela, victim of the 'haunting' I had told her friend about several years ago. She filled me in on macabre events that had taken place during a period spanning eighteen years of marriage. I believed every bizarre event she related to me.

Angela and her husband Steve came from a cultural background that frowned on love marriages. Marriages were arranged by the parents! Steve's mother had found a girl she felt would be a suitable wife for her only son. Steve, however, had fallen in love with Angela and defied his mother's wishes by marrying her. His mother refused to attend the wedding. Steve and his bride immigrated to Canada and shared a happy married life. He was a successful surgeon and they lived in a lovely home where they entertained a large circle of friends.

Two years after their marriage, his mother came to Canada for a visit. It was not pleasant. She constantly chastised him for marrying Angela. She was critical of her housekeeping, clothes, food and friends. She berated her in front of her husband and their friends. Six weeks passed miserably and slowly before she returned home.

Later in the year, Angela became pregnant and delivered a daughter. Her mother-in-law arrived for the event. She was sour as ever. She behaved so badly that friends, fearing for the well-being of the new mother, persuaded her to return home.

Two years later a second daughter was born to the happy couple. Again, Steve's mother soured the couple's life with a visit. She was more vicious now than she had been earlier. She visited all her son's friends and complained bitterly about Angela, insisting her son was not happy and that she wasn't the right woman for him. Nothing less than a divorce would satisfy her. She was oblivious to the fact that her son was happily married. She returned home and it was five years before she again visited her son and his family. Five years during which they had been very content.

This visit brought disaster. Angela was again pregnant, but within two weeks of her mother-in-law's arrival, she miscarried. Her daughter-in-law's misfortune did not touch her heart. She cruelly blamed Angela for the loss of the baby. Steve insisted that his mother return home. She raged, screaming and cursing them both before she left.

Steve and Angela became the parents of a beautiful boy the following year and Steve's mother, now a new grandmother, came to visit. This time her behavior was so outrageous that Steve escorted his mother back to her country. The next several years passed peacefully. Steve and his mother maintained contact through the telephone and by letters during this period.

Suddenly, she arrived at their door. It was to be a memorable visit. A series of mishaps befell Angela. She suffered another miscarriage. She fell on her face in her driveway and cut it so badly she needed stitches. She burned her thigh with boiling fat so severely that it required medical attention.

A sliding glass closet door fell and narrowly missed Angela. It smashed to the floor in many pieces. Her car mysteriously caught fire twice as she was driving, once while she was on top of a bridge. The most difficult situation for Angela to deal with was her husband's changed personality. He became abusive toward his family. The children were a source of irritation to him and he now beat his wife. His outrageous behavior caused his wife and children to ask him and his mother to leave the home. Steve moved into an apartment and his mother returned to Yugoslavia. She died within a month of returning home.

Steve left for Yugoslavia to attend to his mother's funeral. Afterwards, he flew to London, England and visited friends because he felt the need for a vacation. He attended a party celebrating an infant's baptism. He was exchanging pleasantries with a priest when the priest broke off the conversation, placed a hand on Steve's shoulder and said, "My son, there's an evil spirit in your house who wants to destroy your marriage. You must have it removed immediately." Already in a depressed state, Steve couldn't deal with the disclosure and put it out of his mind.

He missed his wife terribly and wanted her with him. His friend placed a call to Angela who, after hearing the friend's account of Steve's state of mind and his expressed desire to have her with him, flew out on the next flight to join him.

Her presence cheered him and they enjoyed their time together in London. A farewell party was held in their honour the evening before they left and the priest was invited to attend. He told both Steve and Angela that the evil spirit must be removed from their home. He insisted their future happiness depended on it. Happily reconciled, they didn't want to think or talk about such a thing.

They returned home and resumed living together. Steve's hostile behavior soon returned and friends tried to bring peace between the couple again. It was here that my name was mentioned. The friend who had seen me reminded Angela of what I had said. The spirit of Steve's mother was 'living' in the house intent on destroying their marriage as she had been during her life. Angela then told her friends the message the priest in London had given them; that an evil spirit lived in their house determined to ruin their marriage. Steve had recently moved out.

Angela sat before me, her story now told and she had a question for me. Had her mother-in-law paid someone in Yugoslavia to 'cast the evil eye' on her? I understood the meaning of the question she put to me. *

I felt the mother-in-law's spirit remained in Angela's house. She could not rest until Angela and the children suc-

---

* The evil eye's origin is lost in time. It's an ancient belief shared by many cultures and races. I've met believers in its powers who came from India, Africa, Hawaii, the Orient, Arabia, Eastern Europe,

cumbed to constant and complete unhappiness.

Now willing to seek help, she asked what could be done to stop this evil. Should she send for the priest in London to end the possession? If she wanted to, yes—or I could do it for her, I offered. She asked what my fee would be. I explained to her that I never accept money or gifts for putting a spirit to rest. I asked her only to have a cup of tea and something sweet for me to eat afterwards, because my energy would be drained and I'd need to rest for a short time.

I stressed it was important that no one else be allowed in the house while I was performing the exorcism. I explained I wanted her near me as I worked because I felt the evil spirit might try to attach itself to Angela personally, as she had its main focus. With her standing near me I could stop that from happening. We arranged a convenient time for my visit to her home to perform the exorcism.

Angela expressed surprise that I had brought nothing with me to use for the rite. She was also visibly nervous. I explained that I had no need for paraphernalia of any kind. I asked her to let me wander where my psychic instincts took me, to observe what was happening, and to follow me closely. No interruptions were allowed. She wasn't to answer the phone or the door. She agreed, looking even more nervous

---

the East and West Indies, Greece and Central, South and North America. I visited the Holy City of Hardwar, situated on the banks of the river Ganges, on a trip to India and saw the little blue eyes in the market stalls. There are those who believe in the evil eye, and that some people have the power to look into another person's eyes and curse them. The belief is that if one wears, or carries, a glass eye or displays it in the home, then evil will never find them. I was aware of this belief, but it wasn't until a trip I took to Jerusalem that I saw how strongly it was believed in. Along the Via Dallaroza, which is the route Jesus Christ walked on his way to His Crucifixion, strings of blue glass eyes hang in the little stalls of the markets. They're found on key chains, rings, necklaces and bracelets. Others are to be pinned to undergarments. Moslems and Christians alike were selling them.

than when I entered the house.

I found my way into the dining room. As my legs began to feel heavy and I felt chilled to the bone, I knew I was close to the evil force. I told Angela the evil spirit 'lived' not in the basement area but on the main floor of the house. She informed me that I was standing over the area her husband had used as a bedroom during the periods they had suffered difficult times.

I found my way, unguided, into the basement area. Instinctively, I stood on the exact spot where her husband's bed had been. I felt such a strong burning sensation run through me—almost like a fire. I was in the presence of evil! I found what I came to find.

I felt the spirit had settled in other areas of the basement as well. I walked to another spot, and again was engulfed by the burning sensation. I told her the spirit was 'alive' here as well. Angela answered that was the exact spot her husband had sat to watch television during their estrangement. (The rooms were bare of furniture as Steve had taken it with him when he moved out.)

I walked to a small washroom and again experienced the fiery sensation travel through my body. I asked Angela to bring three plants to me. She complied. I placed one in each area that I felt the evil spirit lived.

I went to work. Raising my arms, I silently willed the spirit to rest. I observed the plant in front of me begin to shake. I had the spirit on the run, but it still wasn't ready to go. It was trying to attach itself to the plant, to live through the plant's energy. I silently addressed the devil, telling him his power in this house was at an end. God was moving in and would remain. I then addressed God, begging him to allow me to completely absorb the evil force and release it to the other world. The leaves of the plant ceased to shimmer and I knew I had succeeded in putting the spirit to rest before it had captured the energy of the plant. This would have allowed it to live and continue to cause harm to the family.

I repeated this procedure in each area that I had felt the burning sensation. In each instance, the spirit reacted in the same manner and tried to attach itself to a plant. Ultimately, I was successful in capturing the evil force and releasing it.

I have a handwritten account from Angela describing the events of my visit. As a postscript, she added that her eldest daughter, during the previous year, had become quite nervous and was having problems sleeping at night. The seventeen-year-old girl suddenly demanded her bedroom light be kept on all night. She was afraid to sleep without it, saying she saw a shadowy figure. During this period she also developed an annoying cough. Steve and Angela would hear her cough from their bedroom. An echo always preceded the cough. They discussed this phenomenon and could find no logical reason for it—an echo in their house—an echo? Why not hear the echo after the cough, instead of before? All this stopped after my visit, Angela wrote. Her daughter was no longer nervous or afraid to sleep without a light on in her room at night. Her cough disappeared, and with it the backward echo. Steve and Angela reconciled, resuming a happy family life.

Chapter 2

Children Will Be Children

Before recounting the following story I'd like to comment on the relation between plants and my work with spirits. Plants are a living, breathing organism. A mass of energy surrounds them as it does with humans. Sophisticated and technically advanced photographic equipment and film allows these energies, or auras, to be photographed. This has led scientists to acknowledge that all objects, both animate and inanimate, are surrounded by a field of living energy.

However, the manner in which I was introduced to this fact involves energy transference. The spirit of the young boy in this story tried to live by entering the living energy of a plant.

Plants have become my report card. When I put a spirit to rest, I closely examine all plants in the area I'm working in. If they remain healthy after I've done my work then I've not successfully put the spirit to rest. If the leaves start turning under, shake, or fall off, this is a sign to me that the spirit is trying to escape me. It's trying to live through the plant, enabling it to further haunt its victims.

I found my introduction to the correlation between the two to be a bit traumatic. I received a phone call from Patricia, who was in great distress.

"Something has been happening in my house for a very long time. My husband, our children, and I have all seen ghosts of children. My two younger sons aren't bothered by them—they think it's neat. David, my eldest son, is being attacked by one. Will you please come and see what you can do?"

Upon arriving at her home I found six or seven children's spirits. Only one was hostile enough to create serious problems that would warrant a call for my help.

I asked Patricia and her husband Michael to follow me as I moved through the house. I wanted them to observe what would be happening around us as I worked to put the spirits to rest. I also asked that they not tell me anything that had been occurring. I'd tell them what had been happening in their home and to their family as I wandered from room to room.

I immediately walked through the living room and up the stairs to David's bedroom describing what had been happening. There had been apparitions at night from an ambiguous spirit. In a way he was friendly, wanting to play with David; in another way he was trying to frighten him. I felt he was a spirit who never had a chance to be a child during his own lifetime—that his own life was cut short. He was envious and resentful of David's youth. The parents had seen their son's toys flung askew around the bedroom as David slept.

When I entered the bedroom the air turned cold. The bedspread and drapes began to move and an extremely cold current of air enveloped me. Digging my heels into the carpet I stood firm as the spirit moved through me. As the air around me started to warm, I felt I had put the spirit to rest. The process had taken about ten minutes.

We started back downstairs. We could suddenly feel a force behind us on the stairs, pushing us down as though to hurry us out of the way. The push concerned me but I was so exhausted I needed to rest. We went into the family room where I lay down.

I listened as Michael and Patricia described what had happened. They quietly described with awe how the pictures on the wall behind me moved, the air turned cold, and the hem of my dress swished back and forth. Suddenly, I bolted upright and said, "I must go into your living room, something is there."

What happened next was a trying experience. If I was ever going to be frightened doing my work, this would have been the time.

They followed me as I walked to a corner where a large plant stood. I felt the most stubborn, hostile force I had ever felt. The plant was shrouded in a bitter, angry field of negative energy. I hadn't previously experienced the phenomenon. The spirit had transferred itself into a living, growing plant. I didn't feel evil, merely anger. The air around the plant turned ice cold, colder than I had ever experienced. I thought, "Oh, my God, I don't know if I can do this." It was so strong!

I took a very determined stance and vowed to absorb the spirit. I was becoming angry. To think that it was so stubborn, so hostile and so determined to stay and continue bothering the child! I stood directly in front of the plant. The feeling within me was extremely heavy, yet I felt I had begun to absorb the spirit. There was something wrong this time. I didn't feel it was lifting because it was going to rest. It was lifting because it was so much stronger than I.

I stood as firmly and as defiantly as I could and willed it to me. I began to feel movement. The hem of my dress began swaying back and forth and my foot began to move involuntarily, inching away from its place beside my other foot. The spirit was putting me off balance, distracting me! With all my energy, I concentrated on removing the force that had now settled around my ankle.

I stood still with my arms raised and fighting with every bit of energy I could. It was my will against the spirit's. I concentrated on the plant. I saw the leaves shimmer. One by one, the leaves began to droop and shrivel, as if relenting. As this happened, I began to feel lightness and warmth around me. I had absorbed the spirit. The spirit had died and so had the plant.

I could barely walk after this experience. I was very weak. Patricia and Michael helped me to the living room where I lay down. They noticed something most startling. On my ankle were white indentations of thumb-prints—proof that something had tried to knock me off my feet!

Patricia and Michael told me that a young boy had lived in the house at one time. He had died of leukemia at nine-years of age. Children love two things: to play and other children.

The above story tells of a child's strong desire to play with other children. The desire was strong enough to transcend death. The little lost soul had been looking for a play-mate and a normal life with other children.

Chapter 3

I Confess

Joan lived seven years with her ghosts before her two daughters confessed to their mother that they had seen the ghost of an elderly woman.

I first entered Joan and Edward's lovely home on a Friday afternoon. They had bought it recently and were anxious for me to see it. When there is a ghost in a home, I walk directly to the area it inhabits. Today was no different. Joan hadn't mentioned unnatural disturbances to me, so I said nothing to her when I felt drawn to a small room facing the beautiful summer garden.

While Joan proudly showed me each room and area of her home, my eyes and thoughts kept returning to the small room. I was eager to go back to it. I wanted to spend time in it. Saying only that my favourite room in the house was the little one facing the beautiful garden that Joan nurtured, I walked back to it while she went to the kitchen to make coffee. Such a feeling of peace and contentment came over me. I felt basked in love. Love not for me, but for the house. It wasn't coming from me, but through me.

An elderly woman with white hair sat in a small rocking chair looking out onto her garden, and this ghost looked very content. Her happiness was contagious and even while I shared her feelings, I also felt that I was an intruder.

Joan served coffee and cake in the living room as we chatted about things of no great importance. I kept an eye on the little room straight ahead of me. The ghost in the rocking chair wasn't leaving. She gently rocked in her chair while looking out onto her garden, even as I left.

Seven years after that visit Joan was paying me a social call when, before leaving, she brought up the subject of ghosts. She confided she'd have felt stupid talking about this to anyone, but she thought she had ghosts in her house. Was it possible, she asked. Not giving me time to answer, she rushed on with an explanation. "I hear an old man and an old lady talking," Joan began. "One rocks while the other sits on the floor. Their voices are a low murmur and they seem engaged in a conversation. I can't hear what they're saying. They continue like this for some time, then it just stops. Sometimes I hear music coming from a radio while they chat. Other times I hear music, the same soft low type of music, without seeing them. It happens mostly during mid-afternoon, although I have experienced this in early morning and evening."*

I offered to come by her house to see what I could pick up. I wasn't ready yet to mention what I had seen. I felt I didn't have the full story on the ghosts and that there should be more information. I asked Joan if her husband had seen or heard anything that could be considered ghostly. She had asked him, explaining what she had experienced. His answer confused her further. No, he hadn't. Yet I felt certain someone else had seen a ghost, or ghosts, in Edward and Joan's home.

---

* People only call me if there's a lot happening. It's rare that I'm asked in on the strength of isolated incidents. Some people fall in love with their ghosts because they have a personality in death the same as they did in life.

Soon after Joan's visit, the courses I give in Reincarnation began and she joined them as a student. We came into contact with each other, and she with others who shared her thoughts on the afterlife. Joan began to talk without feeling foolish about her ghostly occurrences. She's a very practical person and, like other people with ghosts in the house felt alienated and different— she thought she looked foolish. It was good for her to be with a group of people who understood her, even if they hadn't had a ghostly experience themselves.

I had directed the students to meditate by concentrating on a question that needed answering. I felt certain Joan's question would be, "When will the restaurant sell?" What had once been a source of both joy and income to the couple was now an albatross around their necks. Their business had been on the market for over a year and they had yet to receive an offer. This wasn't in keeping with what was happening in the business community. Sales had been brisk. The price was so reasonably set that it might lead a prospective buyer to wonder why it was so low. They wanted an early retirement while still in good health, and they had travel plans. I observed Joan while she was deep in meditation and sensed a breakthrough. An answer was coming and it was being given in a different language.

As I directed my students out of their state of meditation, Joan appeared very calm. I left the room to make coffee while the class wrote an account of their meditation travels.

While I served refreshments, each student told of their experiences. When Joan's turn came, she began by telling us she had been sitting in her restaurant, not as it was today, but as it was during the time of its original owner. I interjected here to inform her she had been speaking in a foreign language, one she didn't use or know. She looked incredulous and, almost gasping, asked me how I could know that the entire conversation was in French!

We all had a good chuckle over this, then listened attentively as she continued. She had been speaking with the ghost of the restaurant's original owner. He was angry and upset that Edward had remodeled his restaurant in such a manner that he could no longer sit in his favourite spot and observe the entire restaurant. Joan could barely restrain herself as she pounded the table and told us she had repeatedly spoken against Edward's determination to erect a wall in a certain area. She just didn't feel it was right. Now she had the answer to why the restaurant wouldn't sell. Its deceased owner was responsible, she insisted.

On different occasions she had felt a presence in the building, telling Edward she thought the former owner was haunting them. I calmed her down by promising that I would visit her restaurant soon.

We sat and chatted at a small table. While I was aware of the conversation, I wasn't giving it too much attention. Something of interest caught my eye. I described him later as someone who looked like a Bulgarian wrestler. He was tall with a large body, hairy hands, round face and a ring of white hair on an otherwise bald head. I felt that he, and not the Frenchman, was interfering with the sale of the restaurant. I left him sitting on a barstool and walked to where Joan's ghost was instead. There I proceeded to put him to rest. It didn't take long to persuade him to leave for his rightful home on the other side! He wasn't malevolent in any way and just a gentle prodding was necessary.

I returned to the bar where I had felt the troublesome ghost. He was still there. I then joined Joan and Edward and informed them of their not too friendly intruder. After a brief ten minute rest, I was ready to tackle him. He was reluctant to move into the other side, he enjoyed the atmosphere of the bar.

I continued, feeling the full force of his negative energies. It took great determination on my part to stay with it. I began to feel that I had been successful in absorbing his energy when I felt I needed to sit down for a few moments. As I sat and rested, I saw him ever so slightly reappear. I gathered my energy and approached him again. It was less stressful now for each of us, as we were each half way to our goal. I could now gently will him to cross over.

Edward left us to pick up needed supplies, but not before I had sprinkled holy water on him. Joan and I talked over a cup of coffee, going over the events of my visit. She said I had described to them the physical appearance of the previous owner when I spoke of the apparition of the Bulgarian wrestler. The man they had bought the restaurant from had looked in life exactly as I had described him to them. We agreed upon a suitable time for me to visit her ghostly couple at their home before I left.

This visit held a different meaning for each of us. Joan was apprehensive because there was a mission involved. I felt quite relaxed as I prepared to go to work. I knew when I had finished my task we'd relax with cake and coffee as old friends do.

Joan had mentioned that she usually heard music and dialogue when she was working in her downstairs office. We went to the lower level of the house. I went from room to room. I told her there was nothing in these rooms, all the activity came from the upstairs area. It was then that I told her what I had seen the first time I visited her home.

She was willing to believe me, yet I sensed a bit of confusion from her because she had always felt they lived downstairs. We returned upstairs. I went to work, slowly and gently calling the loving couple to me. They came without reluctance. I released their energy, allowing them to take their place in their own world.

I had again taken the bottle of holy water with me out of respect for Joan's religious roots. I sprinkled some around the little room facing the garden. Joan had admired the container and wanted to know where she could buy one like it. I was visiting a Shrine that week and said I'd be happy to pick one up for her.

I returned to Joan's Sunday evening with the much appreciated bottle of holy water. She had a surprising disclosure for me. When her two daughters paid a visit the previous day, she relayed to them the events that led to my Friday visit. They each had a story to tell their mom, one they had kept to themselves and not even shared with each other for seven years.

The eldest daughter was sitting in the living room shortly before her marriage, when she suddenly saw the ghostly figure of an elderly white-haired lady standing in the garden. This, she informed her mother, was the reason she had refused to sleep in a main floor spare bedroom. It looked out onto the garden.

No doubt there is strength in numbers. This exposé encouraged Joan's younger daughter to confess as well. While pregnant with her son, the expectant mother had fallen asleep on the living room couch one afternoon. She awakened with a start, not knowing why.

The reason was gliding across the living room. The figure of a short, elderly white-haired lady moved past her towards the small room looking out onto the garden, and disappeared.

There's also another ghost, a younger girl in her early twenties, dressed in the style of the early 1920s. It was summertime and she had a straw hat on. This girl was standing in a cornfield.

Ten years later this same girl came back as a fourteen-year-old and I felt she was mourning a young man who had gone off to war and was killed. A friend of mine who is a researcher told me that there used to be a cornfield that crossed all the way across the highway by the house. I was now satisfied that my feelings of seven years ago had been corroborated.

Chapter 4

While Angels Sleep

The subject of babies causing paranormal phenomena isn't often discussed in literature. This is because it is a rare and limited number of infants who cling to the present. Newborn babies don't form materialistic attachments or cling emotionally to people in particular during their early months of life. They willingly accept love and comfort in anyone's arms.

The habits children and adults acquire with time that are not an integral part of their nature are the reason we can have a little lost soul clinging to the life state—a baby ghost.

I had wrapped up my radio call-in show and was heading home when the receptionist handed me a message. I glanced at it briefly, only partly concentrating on its words. When I spotted the word baby I gave it my full attention.

Early that afternoon I dialed the number given in the note. A young voice answered. Since there was no name of reference on the brief message, I introduced myself and said

I was responding to a message left for me at the radio station.

"I heard you talk about ghosts on your show this morning." A listener had called in to discuss the subject. I remembered the call. The woman had been upset by a playful presence in her kitchen for several years, but it had not bothered her over the past several months. We talked about whether the ghost was gone for good, and the time it took for a ghost to disappear.

"You told her that it was probably gone for good, and that a ghost could be around for years unless it was put to rest by a professional."

"That's right," I answered.

"You even told her over the radio what her ghost had been doing. It was moving and hiding things, it changed the time on the clock, and emptied her dishwater."

"Yes, I felt the ghost had done these things and the caller corroborated it for us," I replied.

"Could you help me?" the young woman asked. Before I could reply she excitedly went on. "There's a ghost in my baby's room." I asked her name and address and arranged a time to inspect her apartment. I impressed upon her that I wanted only the baby and her husband present with her.

"Does it matter if my husband isn't here, he's working afternoons?"

"That would be fine as long as no one else is present," I said.

She agreed to place a few plants in the baby's room before my visit. I also told her that I didn't want any information upon my arrival at the apartment—she was only to follow me closely and observe. She assured me that she understood, and I gave her my assurance that her baby was in no danger.

"There's a mobile hanging above your baby's crib, and its music wakes you and your husband during the night," I said.

"My God, how did you know?" she whispered, unbelievably.

"I'll see you soon, Debbie."

It was a high rise apartment building in central St. Catharines, Ontario. The apartment that would hold my interest and have my undivided attention was situated on the main floor. I rang the buzzer and Debbie's voice answered on the intercom. She released the automatically locking door after I identified myself.

Debbie was in her early twenties. Dressed in jeans and a tee shirt she could have passed for a high school student. Her face showed apprehension and strain. She was fidgety in her nervousness. "Najla, is anything going to happen to my baby?" Debbie asked anxiously.

"Absolutely not!" I assured her, putting my arm around her shoulder.

"What do you want to do first?" the young mother asked.

"I'd like to sit here," motioning to a chair in the living room, "and I'd like you to relax and listen to what I have to say before I go into the baby's room." I could see how difficult it was for her to relax as she gingerly sat down on the pretty floral chesterfield.

"Debbie," I began, "your son's toys have been found helter-skelter around his room as he sleeps, both during the day and at night." She started to respond to my statement, but I held up my hand to indicate that I had more to say. "There's one stuffed toy in particular that's moved around more than other toys, and usually you find it in a drawer of the baby's dresser."

I continued as she stared at me, "You enter his room to find articles moved and even tossed to the floor. The most traumatic incident is the moving mobile," I said. I let her talk then.

"My husband didn't believe me at first," she began. "He was baby-sitting one evening while I was out shopping.

When I came home he looked stunned and told me something was definitely happening in the baby's room."

The two month old infant was sleeping soundly when his
father looked in on him. Returning to the television set, he
settled down to relax. The sound of the musical mobile playing its pretty lullaby led the attentive dad to think the baby
was kicking in his crib. He headed down the hall to get his
son.

The sight greeting his eyes convinced him to agree with
his wife. Something strange was happening in their son's
room. The infant was sleeping soundly, but it looked like his
room had been played in. Toys were strewn on the floor and
the mobile was moving. Stunned, the young man picked up
his sleeping son. He checked the mobile. It was wound tight.
'Impossible,' he thought. It had automatically wound down
after playing itself out. He had placed his son in the crib and
left the room after winding the mobile tight. He had heard it
play itself out!

Wondering if he should he go into the room to rewind it,
he looked in on his sleeping son and decided not to. Now
the mobile was playing like it had during the night, he
thought. He had tried to convince his wife there was a logical explanation for the sounds coming from their son's room.
He realized there was no logical reason.

Sitting in the living room, holding his son close to him,
the disturbed father prayed to God to keep his son safe.
There had been another baby. Their first-born was lost due
to an unexplained crib death. Would they lose another, he
wondered worriedly.

Coming home from her shopping trip Debbie found her
husband was anxious to talk about what he had earlier put
out of his mind. He had touched nothing in the baby's room
and holding his son in his arms, he asked his wife to accompany him to the scene of the disturbance.

Debbie was frightened, yet relieved at the sight greeting

her eyes. "Do you believe me now, Roger?" she asked her husband. During the following weeks the unexplained events were repeated. The mobile played without human hands winding it while toys continued to be tossed around the room on a frequent basis. Debbie and Roger's anxiety grew and with it their feelings of helplessness. The following Tuesday morning she was tuned into my radio show and heard the conversation which prompted her to contact me.

Now I was here and ready to go to work. I walked down the hall to the sleeping infant's room, with Debbie following me closely. I stood in the doorway and sensed a presence hovering over the baby's crib. The room was uncharacteristically warm—it basked in warmth. 'Not your average spirit,' I thought. The cold draft that accompanies a spirit was missing replaced instead by a warm one. The purity of the entity was overwhelming. I felt love, comfort and protection emanating from it. 'So, it's a baby ghost,' I thought, gazing around the room. The plants Debbie had placed around the room were moving lightly, as though a gentle breeze was blowing on them. With the baby in the crib sleeping, I exorcised the infant spirit of his brother.

Talking to the entity as I would an adult ghost, I gently convinced it to leave the company of its brother. I impressed upon him that he had made the decision to quit this lifetime, and he should abide by his choice. I turned to leave, motioning for Debbie to follow. We returned to the living room, where I accepted her offer of a cup of coffee. I knew how anxious she must be to ask me what I had picked up in her son's nursery. Once coffee was served and she was seated, I explained the situation to the anxious mother.

I told her that crib deaths are considered a medical phenomenon, Spiritually speaking, they're caused by an infant's desire to return to the state of Bardo—the state we all enter before incarnating on the earth plane. It is a state of spiritual development.

She listened attentively as I explained reincarnation to her. I said that we all have a preview of the life we are planning to enter, and that sometimes a newborn soul chooses to return to the other side to learn more from the Master Teachers. They simply change their mind and return later. I had opened a new door of thought for her. Her silence was a sign of contemplation and I knew many questions would be tumbling forth from the young mother as a result. "Do you mean my baby is really my first son?"

"No, not at all." I assured her. "Your first son is the ghost that has been creating the playful and harmless disturbances," I continued. "After deciding he wasn't willing to live the life he had chosen, he died." Between the death state and entering Bardo, he decided he wasn't quite ready to depart and a ghost was created. He's been hanging around your baby in a playful manner. I've convinced him to cross over to the other side and I'm certain you'll have no further unsettling incidents."

"If I have another child, will it really be my first baby," Debbie asked, trying to grasp the concept of reincarnation.

"No, it won't. Your first baby decided to make a brand new start when he left you and his father," I explained. "You won't have contact with that little soul again," I assured her. "Not as a baby or a ghost."

Slowly she relaxed. My work was done. Upon taking my leave I told her to call me if she had any further questions, or if her husband wished to speak to me about the incidents and our ensuing conversation. I don't do follow up work. I leave it to the people involved to contact me if there are further disturbances. Since I've not heard from Debbie and Roger, I assume all is well, as I expected it would be.

Chapter 5

More Than She Asked For

Anita's ghost hung around out of admiration for her. She lived through Anita. Susan had died at a young age after living a humiliating and painful life, where she was tortured both physically and emotionally. Through hanging around with Anita she could partake in an enjoyable and comfortable lifestyle. Her demise came only because she unwittingly accompanied her unappreciative counterpart to my office. The following is Anita's account of her ghostly experiences and subsequent release from them, written to me in a letter:

"Dear Najla,
I'd like to apologize for being late with this letter.
You truly amazed me when I came to see you for a psychic reading in the spring. During the reading you told me

that we had a spirit in the house that I'm presently living in. I smiled because I felt this was true, because of what I'd been experiencing. My sister Connie also felt there was a presence in the house.

My sister often said to me that it seemed she saw someone flitting by her out of the corner of her eye. On one occasion when she was alone in the house, she heard a voice call her name from downstairs. She replied, went down to welcome her guest, but no one was there. This has happened to her on a few occasions.

My own experiences were of a different nature. One night I came home very late, about 3:00 a.m. The house was completely dark. I went to the dining room and turned on the light. I heard three knocks next to the staircase door leading to the basement. I thought it was Connie, but when I opened the door there was no one there.

I couldn't sleep once on a very dark, heavy and warm night. I suddenly felt as though I were going into convulsions. (The spirit was trying to possess Anita.) My body jerked crazily and I heard a woman's voice. She was crying loudly, but I couldn't make out her words. This distressed me because she sounded so unhappy and disturbed. The feelings subsided eventually and I spent a few extra hours awake with the lights on.

As you and I spoke, Najla, the most amazing thing happened. The beautiful and full plant next to me began to wilt in front of my eyes. The leaves turned under and began to sag. Najla, you told me that her spirit was with us and described her as being a young girl who was either orphaned or abandoned and very unhappy. You felt her name was Susan, and that she had once lived on the premises years ago (not necessarily in the house, but on the acreage). You said that she received room and board from two men living there and in return she'd do farm chores. You also said Susan was sexually abused by both men during the time she spent with them. As a result, she became very unhappy and distressed. Susan contracted lockjaw while tending the farm animals and died some time later. Najla, you said she didn't accept her death which explained why we were experiencing her presence.

Susan also made her presence known to my by using other methods. I'd be watching television when suddenly it would click off. All the lights would be on but the television wouldn't work. Someone else would turn it on and it would work for them. This aggravated me because it was usually during a show I longed to see.

You told me that Susan had a liking for me. She liked my independence and was drawn to me as a friend. She wanted to share my life. You thought perhaps. I could speak to her and let her know during one of the occurrences that it was time for her to move on, that she was dead. I'd not look forward to this.

You said you'd try a long distance exorcism. You were quiet for a few minutes and I continued to observe the sagging plant. After you finished concentrating you said you felt she might have gone but you hadn't done a long distance exorcism before and asked that I contact you if I felt Susan was still around me. You'd come to the house if necessary. Najla, since then I've felt no presence in the house and my television stays on. Your exorcism must have worked and I am grateful.

I'd like to add another thing in this letter. I recently had another reading with you. Connie was telling me after the reading that she felt we had another spirit. She has heard something fall in the house with a loud thud on several occasions. She suspected it was a door closing but found no doors closed. Nothing had fallen onto the floor. We may need to call you, Najla. I'll keep in touch. As for me, I've experienced nothing further."

* * * * * *

Anita came to my office for a psychic reading and experienced an exorcism, much more than she asked for.

The thudding sounds Connie continued to hear were obviously attached to the house, which is why they persisted after I successfully slipped Susan into her proper dimension.

CHAPTER 6

A Full House

Ruth Bronson is in her mid-forties, a mother of four daughters and a teacher of children with learning disabilities. The longevity of her unwanted ghostly house guests would lead most to wonder why she waited so long before asking for help to rid the family home of the unwelcome intruders.

Conditioning is difficult to overcome. Ruth is a devout Roman Catholic who follows the teachings of the Church, which stipulate that she not believe in any type of psychic phenomena. It would be difficult for her to approach a priest and ask for help with something she wasn't supposed to believe in. Although the Roman Catholic Church does have rites of exorcism, it is very difficult to find a priest who will do a serious investigation. Even if conclusive proof is established, it is just as hard to get the church's hierarchy to grant permission for the exorcism rite.

Already filled with insecurity created by the intimidating situation at hand, it would be doubly difficult to face yet another situation that may leave her with no hope at all. Where to look for help? She didn't know. This is why for twenty years the Bronson family of London, Ontario lived with an astonishing assortment of ghosts.

The following narrative comes from a recorded account sent to me by Ruth Bronson, who now lives in Halifax, Nova Scotia:

"I can't believe how upsetting it is to go back and remember the twenty years we spent at our London home. We first moved in when our little girls were seven, six, and one-and-a-half-years old. We weren't in the house very long when our seven year old started seeing three different things that bothered her. I guess you'd call them spirits. All three were dressed in very old fashioned clothes. There was a lady with white hair who wore a long dress and left messages with my daughter to finish her homework.

There was a male ghost with white hair who dressed in white, and a soldier who seemed different from the other two. He walked through walls and paced up and down the halls. On several occasions he left coins and once he left a medal. This activity happened in an upstairs back bedroom. The man and lady with the white hair didn't upset my daughter Linda who felt that they were loving and comforting. The child became quite upset by the soldier and mentioned it to her father. His reaction wasn't comforting. He told her she was being silly and there were no such things as ghosts. She was to call him if she thought she saw them again.

She called him one night when she saw the soldier. Her father entered the room and claimed to see nothing, yet Linda saw the soldier walk right through her dad and saw him shiver as though he had a cold chill. Linda no longer saw the apparitions when she got older."

(Children are very receptive to the spirit world. They are very aware of previous lives. When children get older they become more involved with the outside world and recall less of the spirit world. Where children are receptive, adults are less so. It's as though some people are forty watt bulbs and some are one hundred watts. The forty watt will let experiences slide by and the one hundred watt will connect. They will see it. Then there are people like me who see it all.)

"Our younger daughter also reported seeing 'a white lady and man' and 'somebody who was always mad.' Children visiting our house saw the white-haired couple and would come down from the upstairs room crying. They wouldn't come back to play.

Linda married and had a son. He was also visited by the ghosts. Family and friends alike didn't want to come to the house with their children. The children would describe exactly what all the others had seen. They didn't say ghosts, they called them people.

Certain times of the year were more upsetting than others to live in the house. I don't know why. I don't know if it's because they died at that time of year or if this is something ghosts do. I only know it was busier at certain times of the year. Small fires started spontaneously in the house during these busier times and always on the same date.*

Years passed. We tried to sell the house often, it just didn't sell. Houses around us were going like hotcakes, we dropped our price. Still, no sale, although it was identical in appearance to all others on our street. It just never, never sold.

The last attempt to sell the house you know about, Najla. I saw you for a reading. You told me the house would sell quickly. I saw houses around us being sold but not ours. I called you and asked you to come out to the house.

When you came, I told you of an experience I'd had in

---

*   I think this is pretty much a natural phenomena because scientists know that illnesses become more frequent in the Spring and Fall. Schizophrenia, manic depression, ulcers, allergies, insomnia, etc. Its a busier time.

the front bedroom. I awoke feeling like I'd been covered with ice cubes. I couldn't breathe, I just couldn't breathe. I felt I was choking. I could see this presence. I felt that whatever was in that house was afraid of change because every time we put the house on the market, their activities became more chaotic. My marriage broke down while we lived in it. My ex-husband became so disturbed by living with these strange happenings he became estranged from all of us. Like the evening I told you about, when I felt I was being ripped apart by a demon in my bed, and the blankets were actually up in the air. It was a really frightening experience. I remember our youngest daughter telling me this thing would touch her hair and then shake her very violently. The eldest girl told of the same experience when she was small.

I must say I had several miscarriages while living in that house. Janice, our youngest daughter, was born in it. Her birth did not come on the expected date but during one of the busier periods, the month of October, which was always an upsetting time in our house. When I carried Janice, the lady with white hair appeared to me and told me not to be frightened. I wouldn't lose this baby. She was only in the house to protect our children because she had lost a child of her own.

You walked into our house and went right to the back room. You seemed to have a sense of where these things were.* You asked me if we had a plant.* You wanted it with

---

* I felt a lot of anxiety when I walked in that house. I saw emptiness, although there was a lot of furniture in the house. The spirits were dominant and would walk through the walls to get to me.

* A plant is a living thing. A ghost is a ghost because it wants to live. A ghost views me as an enemy because I can contact it and pass it onto the other side. It senses a battle of the wills and will latch onto another living entity to survive. When I come into contact with a ghost it feels its life ebbing away. This is why a ghost will choose a plant. It will try to live in the plant until I'm out the door and it can continue doing what its been doing all along. The ghost is on the other side resting when any plants in the room are shriveled and dead.

us. We went upstairs to the back room and when we went in the room, you stood there concentrating. I felt you were so far away from me. I'm sure you weren't aware of my presence or anything else around us. The leaves on the plant wilted. It didn't seem to take you that long to remove the spirit. Then we went to the front room where I'd had that awful experience. Again, I felt you were in some type of trance—you were gone. I felt you weren't aware of me. The plant's leaves appeared to shake. You seemed to be very cold and shivered, you shook. You seemed to have all the strength drawn out of you. You spent a lot of time in there and you later went back to it to make sure that whatever was up there was gone. Then you went through the house and stopped wherever you felt something. You seemed to be absorbing it.

We then sat and chatted for a while and you told me what you had seen. It was exactly what the children had described to me so many years ago—the very same spirits.

Eleven days after your visit, we had a feasible offer on the house. I must say now that we had received previous offers but they were all very low and all from people with young children or expectant parents. It seems that the spirits only wanted families with children in the house. I accepted the offer that came after your visit and, during the March break I had from my teaching job, I flew to Nova Scotia and bought a beautiful little house.

I spoke with you briefly before we left and told you that I felt a chill in that front bedroom until the day we left, but we did get out, thanks to you.

I can never thank you enough for freeing us from that house. We're so happy here, it's like paradise on earth. It must warm your heart to know all the good you are doing."

Chapter 7

Like Mother Like Daughter

The phone call came on a Friday afternoon. I had been expecting it for two years. Cameron has been a client for many years and occasionally I'd feel him want-ing to contact me. I discarded the feeling thinking that if he wanted to reach me he could do so easily, although I had moved since his last appointment with me. I was happy to hear from Cameron because both he and his wife, Dianne, are a young, energetic and forward-looking couple with worthy ambitions.

While he began to explain how he had been searching for me the last few years, I could only hear in my mind, 'baby, a baby, it should be all right, it will be all right.' Ultimately, it was—but only after a bizarre experience tak-ing us across the ocean to the West Indies and spanning three generations of a very disturbed and fragmented family. It would also call for the help of a Monk in Trinidad and myself.

Let me go back in time to offer an explanation that can

be followed with relative ease. When I first did a psychic reading for Cameron in 1985, one of the statements I made to him concerned his father who was a teacher in Trinidad. His strength of character and integrity impressed me and I felt that he was a God-fearing person. His father was also very lonely. Cameron appeared uncomfortable when I mentioned his father and during all later readings his reaction never varied. His attitude left me puzzled for he obviously didn't feel a closeness to his father, which I felt he should have because of the man's love and devotion for his son.

The puzzle was solved four years later.

There was apprehension, fear and relief in Cameron's voice as he began to explain why he had been so desperate to find me. His wife Dianne was pregnant for the third time, the first two pregnancies had ended tragically after seven months. The doctors could offer no medical reasons. In each instance the babies were perfectly formed and all tests, including ultra-sound, had shown a normal fetus during pregnancy. Why were they delivered dead? Understandably the expectant father was in need of an answer. Dianne was now five-and-a-half months pregnant and he was very anxious.

I measured my words carefully for I sensed a danger, yet I knew this child who concerned him so much now would be fine. I told him that the first two had been little girls and this would be a boy. His relief could be felt over the phone lines. He confirmed that I was right. They had lost two daughters and the ultra-sound test had shown Dianne was now carrying a son. He then asked a question whose answer would have me fighting invisible, evil, and murderous forces.

"Najla, is my mother responsible for Dianne losing the babies? Did she do something when she went to Trinidad that would hurt her?"

I had to answer, "Yes, Cameron, she did." It wasn't an answer I wanted to give, but, realizing the situation must be dealt with, I gave it. He then asked if I felt there was an evil spirit in the house intent on harming Dianne. Again, I had to answer yes. He then pleaded with me to visit their home to see if I could help ease the effects of the occurrences that had robbed his wife of sleep and driven them out of their home and into a rented hotel room.

I asked him to pick me up on his first free day, which happened to be the coming Sunday. I'd never have the physical strength to do my work and still drive the two hours from my home to theirs. He readily agreed to drive me. I again assured him his son would be born healthy and alive, and that his wife would be fine.

Sunday found a very tired Cameron at my door. He had bought a building in Toronto and was converting part of it into a restaurant and leasing the rest to other business concerns. He managed a large recreational complex on the waterfront and pursued other real estate ventures as well. Being forced out of his home and into a hotel room by a menacing force didn't make him a happy expectant father-to-be.

We set out immediately for Toronto to meet his wife who was now at his sister's home awaiting our arrival. We talked as we travelled. I told Cameron what I felt was in the house. A force was trying to smother Dianne, to choke her—something didn't want her to have this baby. I felt he had seen a presence himself and then I straight out told him it was his grandmother who was responsible for the evil that permeated their home. He looked shocked and said he thought that it was his mother who was the cause.

I explained further. His mother's mother had travelled on a yearly basis back to her homeland since moving to Canada from Trinidad and she practised black magic while there. Now in her eighties with failing eyesight and too old to concentrate, she was finding it difficult to carry out her black rituals and had transferred her black art secrets to her daughter—Cameron's mother. He was quite shaken and told me that I was just unreal.

On Thursday, the day before his call found me, he had called his mother to his office and accused her of doing exactly what I had just described to him. She tearfully denied any knowledge of his accusations. He then pulled a gun from his desk drawer and, placing it on his desk, told her that he would use it to kill her if anything happened to either his wife or the expected baby. Now I asked him to explain to me the circumstances that had led to such a painful and desperate confrontation. I was deeply troubled by his actions because his behaviour was such a departure from his usual good natured, respectful approach to people.

Here is the story he related to me.

Earlier in the week Cameron had received a phone call from his father who lives in Trinidad. He had been aware of his estranged wife's recent visit to their home town and had a hunch she'd be up to no-good. He contacted people in the area who would know of the woman's movements and learned what he had suspected was indeed a fact. She had been to see someone reputed to work in the art of black magic. Rumours had reached him about his son's misfortune in the loss of the two baby girls and the concerned father wasn't convinced an act of nature had caused the tragedies. Insight led him to take a trip to the mountains of Trinidad where an order of monks lives secluded from the rest of the world.

There he found willing listeners to his tale of terror. A ceremonial service was held to lift the effects of the black magic.* However, after performing the ceremony of exor-

---

* Natives of Trinidad are accustomed to dealing with the occult and in many homes daily rituals are performed to keep evil spirits away from the house and its inhabitants. It can be an act as simple as sprinkling salt around the outside of the house or it can be as complex as visiting a local person known to practice what they call OBEA—the occult.

cism and talking further with Cameron's father, the priest said that unless someone living closer to his son and daughter-in-law in Canada could do the same as he had, it would result in Dianne being dead within forty-eight hours. He explained that since Cameron's mother took the OBEA to Canada, it had to be dealt with on a personal level.

This was why they were frantically searching to find me. He found my phone number after calling the surrounding areas I had lived in, and wasted no time in asking for my help.

As I listened to Cameron tell this drama while we drove to Toronto, I felt very pleased that I had accurately picked up his father's personality. He had known early in his marriage that his wife and her mother were dealing with occultists and had seen first hand the devastating effect it had on people's lives. His belief in God had caused him to leave his family. He knew that if he took the children from his wife great harm could come to him and them. He bought a small home some distance from them that gave him an opportunity to watch them grow up, although there was no contact. It was now, after years of feeling alienated from his father, that Cameron could comprehend why the man had left his home and family. It also answered why I had said to him that I absolutely loved his father at the time of his first reading, and would like the opportunity to meet such a good man.

I asked him to explain everything from the very beginning, starting with his wife's first pregnancy. Cameron felt it all began on a Sunday afternoon when his mother called Dianne asking her to attend a *puja* (a religious service

---

This involves elaborate rituals and the use of powders, spices, animals and substantial financial payment. The religious order of monks, living on their hill monastery, often receive requests for their intervention to lift a curse placed on a loved one by these dealers of black art. These priests then perform an act of exorcism.

where prayers are offered to celebrate a happy event, or to ask for special favours). Almost immediately disturbances began occurring around their home.

Dianne found it impossible to sleep at night. She felt a presence hovering over their bed, accompanied by a smothering sensation. Soon she was feeling a presence in other areas of the house, including unaccountable noises. She began staying away during the evenings her husband was at work because she no longer felt comfortable in the house. During the day she went to her job as a computer operator and afterwards she'd go to her sister's home until her husband picked her up to retire for the night. Dianne and Cameron both suffered depression resulting from lack of sleep and stress caused by the unknown intrusion. These occurrences eventually became a nightly ritual. Husband and wife would be awakened by a sense of somebody hovering over their bed after falling asleep. A bitter feeling of hostility accompanied the presence.

As Dianne's pregnancy progressed, the disturbances became stronger and more frequent until one night Dianne awoke struggling desperately with something that was trying to strangle her. Dianne's desperate movements awoke Cameron. He turned the light on and to his amazement and horror saw red welts and swelling on his wife's neck. Sleep was now impossible. Wondering if someone was responsible for an OBEA, they skeptically searched the house to see if they could find any signs. The following morning they found powders and spices used in Trinidadian black magic rituals sprinkled around the outside of their home.

Who would commit such a heinous act against them they wondered? They moved out of their home immediately, but living in a hotel room wasn't the answer. What to do? Cameron had suspected his mother's mother dealt in the black arts, but to even think it! He went to his office the following day and began to look for signs such as he had found around their home. He found them in his desk drawers. He next checked an overcoat he had hanging in the office. There, inside the lining, he found packets of the same powders and spices sewn firmly in place on the inside seams. How? He knew an employee of his was a boarder at his mother's home and Cameron wondered if he had taken the coat and returned it unnoticed. Questioning the man brought only denial. He wondered now if his own mother was under the influence of her mother; they had lived together since immigrating to Canada. Could it be possible? And if so, why? Why would anyone want to harm them and their lovingly awaited baby so desperately? Lying in bed in their hotel room that night, they talked about it endlessly. He had tried to find me again that day. Then his father's phone call came and the search to find me intensified.

We arrived at his sister-in-law's home to pick up Dianne. I was heartsick at her trapped look. Her normally very beautiful face was drawn and it was obviously hard for her to force a smile. We hugged and I tried hard to comfort her. Dianne had gone to hell and back twice and she was headed there for a third time. I knew that I could help. I patted her little round tummy and offered words of encouragement. I assured her both she and her unborn child were going to be absolutely fine.

How could I know this? Good and evil have fought since the beginning of time. The art of black magic is evil. Evil is but a thought, a feeling, a wish, a desire or a passion. Thoughts have wings, they travel—which is why we're able to pick up on the feelings of other people and can know when someone is thinking about us, or who will be on the other end of the line when the phone rings.

Evil is thought transference, or telepathy. Some people are so insecure that they can only console themselves by controlling others. The more insecure they are, the greater the need to control. Hence, a person with a minimal conscience gains great satisfaction manipulating the minds of others. It's simply done through thought transference.

There is no need of magic potions, powders, animals, dolls, objects or paraphernalia of any sort. Practitioners of this black art do it for a hefty price. The fear they instill in their customers allows their demented minds to accept it as a show of respect. The driving factor that motivates someone to place a curse on someone else is selfishness. They want someone or something badly enough to pay a great sum of money and to humiliate themselves before the occultist. Since they are not able to attain their desires in an ordinary manner, the avenue they take is this very dangerous one.

Cameron's mother had followed in her mother's footsteps and used these means to control her family. Each had been successful. The marriages of the grandmother's sons and daughters had ended disastrously. When a marriage failed, each child went back to their mother's home to live. Cameron's brother's marriage ended on the honeymoon. He went home again to live with his mother. An uncle of Cameron's had re-married after thirty years of single life. Within three months the marriage was over. Throughout the entire family, the story was the same. There was no sign of happiness for any of its members.

Why? How? How to explain this to anyone who has a conscience and a caring heart. How can anyone who feels love and compassion comprehend and deal with such heinous deeds? I don't feel understanding is possible. Accepting it allows us to deal with the feelings of hate, anger and disgust that rise to the surface when realization sinks in. How can we accept evil? By realizing it exists. There will always be selfish and loveless humans who will want control over others. Absurd as it sounds, parents are most often the guilty parties in these matters. Think about it. If you weren't fond of someone, would you want to keep them in your life? Most often it is a mother who will pay for the services of a black arts dealer. They are afraid of being lonely and alone, and have no feelings of self-worth unless they are in control of their children's lives. These women go to great lengths to keep them ever-near.

If such evil didn't exist, then recognized and legitimate religions wouldn't have their own antidotal ceremonies to counteract this dangerous practice. Prayers of exorcism are known to priests and ministers alike. Although not talked about, these services are carried out today.

How is an exorcism done? With goodness, pure thoughts, and through prayers. A winged prayer travels and finds the evil thoughts and wishes. The good overtakes the evil and the battle ends.

Sound too simple? It is simple! What could be easier, more natural or comforting than prayer? The mystery is that there is no mystery! The weak-minded individual who seeks out a procurer of curses is in awe of the black magic practitioner. This awe allows these leeches a thriving business.

Over the years many people have approached me asking to remove a curse they feel has been placed on them. I tell them there is no such thing as a curse—which is quite true. Evil thoughts exist that people can counteract, yes, but a curse, no. I tell them also to *never* give money or a gift of any kind to anyone claiming to lift a curse. What can an individual do? Pray—at home, in a church, alone, or with someone else. Simply pray for strength, courage and peace of mind.

Talk to a clergyman. Ask him/her to pray for you and with you. Have a prayer service said for your peaceful intentions. There's a comforting feeling when one looks at a glowing candle. Light a candle at home or in a place of worship. Talk to God as you would a best friend, have a conversation with Him. Good will overtake evil and your prayers will be answered.

The priests in Trinidad know this and therefore told

Cameron's father to contact someone who is accustomed to working in this area. Cameron contacted me knowing I have put spirits to rest. He hadn't spoken with a priest about this although he had the name of one living in Toronto. They both felt more comfortable working with me instead of a stranger.

We arrived at their home and I went to work immediately. As I stepped inside the vestibule, I was appalled by a very strong stench, unlike anything I had previously experienced. There was no obvious reason for the foul odour as the house appeared to be impeccably clean. Yet I smelt what I can best describe as a dead fire together with a sense of dampness.

I asked to be left alone and able to wander wherever my instincts took me. Since I didn't know the home, they felt they should lead the way. I asked them only to follow me and observe. We would sit and discuss things later.

I walked through the split level house, directing myself to the master bedroom. I stopped briefly to glance at an empty bedroom on my left and commented that only good would ever come from the room. I felt there had been no happenings in it. Dianne said that they had chosen that room for the nursery out of the four bedrooms in the house.

Entering their bedroom wasn't pleasant. A terrible chill hung in the sun-filled room. I touched the side of the bed Dianne slept on and said the bed had to be thrown out immediately. The evil force had attached itself to it. I could see a cloud whirling over her side of the bed and there was an indentation on her pillow. I felt very heavy and extremely cold, as though I couldn't move if I needed to. I knew now I was facing the evil force.

I began to rid the house of its evil occupant. I felt very focused, supremely grounded and in touch with God. I felt a connection opening between myself and a greater power. I was determined to act as a shield between Dianne and Cameron. I was aware of their anxiety and tried not to upset them any more.

Raising my hands in the air, taking deep breaths and by talking to it, I was able to dismember it. I literally willed it to be gone and after about ten minutes I knew it was. The plants in the room had died, the temperature had risen and a feeling of comfort was in the once uninhabitable bedroom.

How did I do it? I don't know! I only know that I'm able to, for reasons only God knows. Why do I do it? It needs to be done! Why have the ability, if not to use it? Am I ever frightened? Definitely not! What is there to be afraid of? The unknown? Once the unknown becomes known it can no longer frighten. Working good against evil cannot be frightening. Ask a clergy member—it only makes us stronger. Is it expensive to have this done? There is no fee. I'll take neither money nor gifts to put a spirit to rest. Have these people not been victimized enough?

We left the bedroom, but before reaching the bottom step, I said that there was another room in the house I had to visit. I asked them to let me find it. I went down into the lower level of the house, walked into a small room facing the back yard, turned to Dianne and told her that she had also experienced strange occurrences in this area. She agreed this is what had occurred. She had seen a man in that room on occasion and any time she would sit to relax for an evening of television watching, the set would turn itself off. She felt that she wasn't wanted in the room. Again, I stood perfectly still, raised my hands and willed the spirit to leave. When I felt the room to be at peace again, we left.

We then headed upstairs to the kitchen to discuss what had happened. I was drawn, however, to a room off the little one we had left. This was a billiard room. Tears filled my eyes. I felt so wonderfully calm. In this room there was a floral fragrance that I can only think came from Heaven. I couldn't identify the flowers that created such a wonderful scent. The fragrance was beautiful beyond description.

Looking for flowers, I saw none. The room was empty except for the pool table. I took this as a personal sign to me that all would be well.

I was exhausted as I always am after putting a spirit to rest. The energy required to do this is tremendous. A noticeable weight loss occurs as I'm absorbing the entity. My watch falls down around my wrist, and a noticeable space appears between my waist and skirt or slacks band. I lose colour, my voice weakens and I'm ravenously hungry. Generally I'm back to feeling strong and normal in about twelve hours. In this case it took more than twenty-four hours.

Finally, we could sit at the kitchen table and discuss the past and present happenings in detail. I looked at the young couple sitting across from me and my joy was great. They would have to deal personally with Cameron's mother and grandmother. I suggested they sever contact. How could they have normal relations? It was out of the question.

I felt they could be quite happy together despite their orchestrated tragedies. Dianne had close family ties with her parents and siblings. Cameron felt the same towards them. I felt reassured that the baby coming into the world would have loving relatives around him.

During our conversation, Dianne mentioned Cameron's grandmother had given the bed to them as a wedding gift. They were most eager to throw it out and destroy it. Their feelings certainly were understandable. I listened as they talked about the pain and suffering of losing first one child and then a second one. Dealing with their suspicions had been agonizing for them. Confronting Cameron's mother with a loaded gun had been a gut wrenching, painful act for him. They were driven from their home by an invisible terror without knowing when, or even if, they would be returning. The emotions they had been dealing with were almost incomprehensible. The phone call from Cameron's father found them in a heightened state of anxiety. His message had struck them with yet more terror. A bitter disappointment arose in the couple when their suspicions toward the mother and grandmother were confirmed. What followed were all-consuming feelings of rage. Finally, we were all talked out and exhausted. We left the house and headed for my home.

I heard from Dianne three months later. She wanted to share the happy news with me. She had given birth to a seven-and-one-half pound son. Mother and son were fine! There had been no further bizarre intrusions into their now very happy home.

CHAPTER 8

THE CAPTIVATING CAPTAIN

One of my favourite encounters with the spirit world happened in the historical town of Niagara-on-the Lake, Ontario. I met Captain Swayze when asked by the host of a local television program to go on a live ghost hunt for a show that she was producing. I was to walk through a few reputedly haunted establishments and relate to the television camera what I was psychically picking up.

The flimsiest of reasons will take me to my favourite little town. This seemed so much more substantial than a flimsy reason and I readily agreed.

Away from the busy streets and throngs of visitors to the quaint little town of Niagara-on-the Lake, sits the Angel Inn, circa 1771. Few tourists converging on this historical town are aware of the activities created by the spirits inhabiting the little Inn.

Florence Le Doux, the past owner, has shared her more than seventy-year-life with Captain Swayze, who was a

British Army Officer during the war of 1812. Her great grandfather first met Swayze, as Florence lovingly refers to the Captain when he bought the Inn in 1823.

Obviously a gentleman, the officer introduced himself by name to Mrs. Le Doux's great grandfather. After the passing of some time, he felt he wanted to know more about Captain Swayze. He wrote relatives of his who lived in England, asking them to research the Swayze family tree.

The results were most fruitful. The co-operative family sent along personal information, including a portrait of Captain Swayze. He had been a talented artist in his lifetime. He was a sculptor, a painter, and was masterful at playing the piano. The self-portrait showed him to be quite a handsome man. It hung at the Inn on a wall for all to admire. It was a wall I didn't like; it upset me to stand close to it.

The crew and I must have presented an unusual sight to its ghostly inhabitants as we noisily entered, carting in everything we'd need to record my psychic reactions while we wandered throughout the Inn. The crew had to rush and set up their equipment because, immediately upon entering the premises, I began to pick up its historical inhabitants, including a few situations.

My instincts directed me to the far left corner of the building. While approaching the area, I felt overcome by a sense of suffering. The feeling intensified as I drew closer. Suddenly, I realized that what I was picking up was coming not from the room, but from below the floorboards on which I was standing.

I felt pain, unnatural pain, caused by torture. Beatings, broken bones, starvation, bloodshed—I felt it all. I also felt the small area wasn't a part of the rest of the Inn. It was different somehow.

My eyes were drawn to a portrait of George Washington hanging on the wall above this particular area. The thought that flew through my mind was it definitely shouldn't be there. I also noticed a portrait of a British officer. As I gazed at the painting I saw the silhouette of two more officers. This told me that all three had suffered the same tortuous fate.

I expressed my thoughts and feelings to the camera before moving onto other areas of the building. I was drawn to one particular bedroom upstairs. I learned later that this was the room Florence had been born in. I turned to a hotel employee and remarked that this was truly a very busy room. I could hear fife and drum music, soldiers were marching and there were beautifully dressed young ladies and gentlemen in army uniforms strolling arm in arm.

The employee agreed, saying that she and many others had heard the music and sensed more than one presence emanating from the room. I reluctantly left the lovely little room and the historical years of the early 1800s.

It was now time for me to meet Florence Le Doux and discuss the events I felt had happened in the Inn. Florence loves her family—family of ghosts that is. She has enjoyed the company of the handsome Captain.

She told us that he has been her constant companion, guardian and friend ever since she can recall. They have had wonderful chats over the years and he has also been her teacher. She informed us with pride that he taught her to paint, sculpt, and play the piano.

Pointing to a portrait of Swayze, she told us that she painted it while his hands guided hers. A well-executed bust of the talented ghost sits proudly on display. Florence tells us Swayze actually molded it using her hands and grey clay she picked up from nearby Fort Mississauga. He told her what type of clay to use and where she'd find it. Florence often treated patrons of the Angel Inn to an impromptu piano serenade. She happily told us that it was Swayze who taught her to play the instrument.

The love and affection she has for this spirited ghost is beautiful to behold. Her face softened into a lovely smile as she related to us years of memorable experiences she has shared with Captain Swayze.

She never opposed discussing her colourful ghostly guests with patrons of the Inn. Heaven knows, she's had to explain them often enough! The spirits are not discreet and entered the bedrooms of overnight guests. Florence recalls that about eighty ladies have complained of a man in red uniform standing behind them in the public washroom. His unwelcome visits were reflected in the washroom's mirror. She became adept at calming jittery tourists and employees alike.

Florence and a visiting psychic were deep in discussion of the ghostly capers happening at the Inn when a waiter overhearing them disclaimed any belief in the paranormal. The psychic challenged Swayze not to let himself be talked about in such a manner, demanding that the Captain show proof of his presence to the waiter. A heavy mug flew from its shelf across the room and hit an oak support beam, leaving a dent that is still seen today. The mug, on its way to hitting the beam, brushed against the waiter's hand and caused it to bleed. The shaken waiter, after he calmed down and was bandaged, admitted that he now believed in ghosts.

As I listened to Florence recount the ghostly occurrences at the Angel Inn, it became clear to me why I felt General George Washington's portrait shouldn't be hung at the Inn. Swayze and his spirited cohorts wouldn't appreciate being reminded of their American captor.

She also pointed out the reason I felt so terribly disturbed as I stood in the small area I first entered. It was the original building built in 1771 and had been used as a prison to house British soldiers captured by the Americans. The cellar beneath it had housed a cell used to confine and, eventually, torture Captain Swayze to death. The building, as it stands today, was built around the original one. This explains why I felt it didn't belong with the rest of it.

Florence has since moved from the Inn and Swayze has followed her to her new home, where he has made himself known to her two-year-old grand-daughter.

CHAPTER 9

PACKAGE DEAL

After recording the ghostly findings at the Angel Inn, we travelled the short distance to Frank Hawley's res-idence. His stately home stands in the town of Niagara-on-the-Lake. It stands today as it did when it was erected in the late 1790s—a lovely white Georgian structure.

The present owner bought the home in the late 1950s. He didn't know it would be a package deal—buy the house and the ghosts come free of charge.

While shopping in the town hardware store a year after the purchase, Frank happened to meet its former owner. By this time more than a few people had mentioned ghostly sightings and Frank half jokingly remarked to the former owner that he hadn't mentioned a thing about ghosts during the transfer of the property. He said that he hadn't because he wanted a sale, and who would knowingly buy a haunted house?

The ghosts of Frank Hawley's historical treasure have been privileged to socialize with illustrious guests. Dinner parties held in the exquisite dining room have been attend-ed by such dignitaries as a Duke of England and a Governor

General of Canada. Is it any wonder that the ghosts remain even after a change of owners?

Frank Hawley isn't a man predisposed to whimsy. He is a noted historian and an inventor of several types of steam engine used in navigation. He spends much of his time traveling as an independent consultant to shipping firms.

We made a noisy entry into his inviting home. Cameras, lights and crew—the necessary equipment to produce a television show. Frank, busy on the phone, motioned us to enter.

I stood in a small, friendly room. My eyes travelled around the room and rested on a huge, natural brick fireplace. Its authenticity impressed me because I recognized it was a cooking appliance. The area meant to contain the necessary wood for a fire was deeply recessed into the fireplace, allowing for a large sized pot to sit over a fire. The wrought iron handle to hold the cooking utensil was still intact.

When asked if I felt anything ghostly. I replied that I felt the room we were in didn't belong to the rest of the house. I said that it hadn't been an addition. It was brought to this spot and placed there as part of the existing home.

With Frank Hawley engaged on the phone, we took it upon ourselves to tour the house. As we walked, I picked up vibrations upstairs, downstairs, and all around the house, including the coach house next to the main house.

The coach house was now used for the servant's quarters and stood vacant. I picked up the spirit of a man living there, dressed in clothing of days passed. I said that he had recently moved an object in one of the rooms.

Entering the formal living room, I saw a young boy and girl beautifully dressed in velvet and lace quietly amusing themselves. There was a sense of reserve about them and I felt them to be ill—lung problems most likely. Then the scene changed and I saw a young woman in her mid-twenties. I felt her to be mischievous, moving articles here and there, now and again.

I also felt that there had been a knocking coming from the back area of the home. I picked this up as we stood in a back room on the second floor. The television host couldn't contain her amazement at this point. She informed me Frank had heard knocking originating from the back door. He thought that someone was using the door knocker but when he opened the door no one was there. This was especially puzzling during his first winter in the house. He would open the door in response to the clacking of the brass door knocker only to find no one there—not even any footprints in the deep snow.

I felt that the dominant spirit of the house was a Civil War soldier. I saw a man of large build, stubborn, and not eager to leave what he felt was his home. He wanted to be master of the house and was antagonistic toward Frank. It was he who kept Frank running to answer his repetitious knocking.

We returned downstairs to join Frank after completing our independent tour of the house. He was now waiting for us in what I called the fireplace room. He had interesting stories to tell us.

The room we were standing in had once been the scullery house. All the cooking was done in it. Kitchen slaves then carried the food to the main house after preparation. It was thought uncouth to have cooking odours in the main house and people of means during the 1800s had a kitchen, or scullery, built at a distance from the main dwelling. This was what I had picked up when I said the room we were in didn't belong to the rest of the house.

Frank and several others have seen an apparition of a young woman appearing to be in her mid-twenties in that room. She would observe them, wrapped in a mist[*] before

---

[*] This mist is ectoplasm which often surrounds a spirit. Though not always visible to the naked eye, it is always present on a photograph of a spirit.

slowly disappearing.

After we finished our interview for the television camera, I asked Frank if I could see the interior of the coach house. Since he had been on the phone when I discussed the moved object, he was unaware of the reason I wanted to view it. When I explained the reason, he seemed surprised, saying that he had been in the apartment the previous day and all had been in order. However, he readily agreed to let me see the coach house.

We entered a beautifully furnished apartment. At first glance everything looked to be in order. Under closer scrutiny I saw the moved object. I pointed to a small table where an empty candle holder was sitting. Beside the holder lay the candle. Pointing to the candle, I said that it had been taken out of its holder. Frank appeared puzzled. He had seen the short candle sitting in its deep holder the previous day.

Satisfied, I reluctantly left another historical dwelling in the old town of Niagara-on-the-Lake.

CHAPTER 10

WHO IS TONY?

Randomly picking up ghosts is done spontaneously, which surprises even myself. While lecturing one winter evening, I accepted questions from the floor. An elderly lady stood and asked if I knew where her grandson was. He had been missing for eighteen months and would now be seventeen years old.

I said, "Who is Tony?"

The grandmother couldn't hold back the tears. "That's his name," she cried. "I'm afraid he's dead," I replied.

After the lecture, she approached me and said she wanted to thank me for putting her mind at rest. The family had all felt that he was dead, but no one would discuss it with her for fear of upsetting her. The heartbroken woman had suffered two nervous breakdowns since his disappearance. She called me the next day to say that she had slept the entire night through for the first time since he had disappeared. She thanked me for putting her mind at ease.

. . . .

"You need this document to settle an estate."

"Yes, I do." I could sense she didn't want to go into details. I told her where to look for it. About three weeks later, a middle-aged man came to me for a private reading. I felt he had suffered a tragic loss through a sudden death. He told me that he had lost his son in a car accident and that his wife had called my radio show hoping I'd be able to help in finding the ownership of the car. They were eager to sell it as it was a constant reminder of the tragedy. The ownership was found where I'd directed the distraught mother to look. Now their son could be buried.

* * * * * * * *

I received a phone call one Saturday morning from a client who was quite upset. Her friend's husband, a sailor, had fallen into the Welland Canal while waiting to board the ship he was sailing. I told her his body would be found within the week. She felt this was unlikely as the lock empties into Lake Ontario. If he had fallen into one of the locks further up between Lakes Ontario and Erie, there would be a better chance of retrieving the body. I said the body hadn't left the canal system and would be found the next week. It was found in Lock Two, the second lock before entering Lake Ontario, exactly the following week.

* * * * * * *

I was headed for the washroom in a quaint little cafe one Saturday afternoon when I felt I should go down a set of stairs to the right of the dining room. There I saw her, wearing a long cotton gingham dress with a white cap and apron. She was about twenty years old, a pleasant spirit just ever so slightly visible. She wasn't up to anything in particular, she just felt comfortable being there. I felt nothing disturbing about her at all. I went back upstairs and didn't mention what I had seen.

About three weeks later, I went back to the same cafe. The owner came to my table. Looking embarrassed and flustered she said, "Don't think me foolish but I've seen the ghost of a young lady in here frequently, so have the waitresses. We feel her sometimes standing beside us when we're serving tables and at other times she stands in the kitchen and just observes. Do you feel anything?" I had to laugh as I explained to her what I had seen on my previous visit. She agreed with me, neither she nor her staff felt disturbed by the spirit. This was a benign spirit who, when she's had enough of wandering, will find her way to the world beyond.

* * * * * * * *

Occasionally it's necessary for me to persuade the living not to interfere in a deceased's life. During the late seventies in St. Catharines, a friend asked me to meet a friend of hers who had recently lost her husband. It seemed she was experiencing great difficulty in accepting his death. The mutual friend asked if I'd drop by for coffee. She would arrange to have the widow over. She explained that it needed to look like an accidental meeting as the woman was uncomfortable about anything concerning psychic phenomena. I understood and agreed.

Her friend was a tiny, fragile-looking lady who was deep in mourning the day I met her. We sat around the kitchen table listening to her tell of her loss and the uncomfortable feelings in her apartment since her husband's death. Sleepless nights resulted from indications of his presence. As I listened, my eyes were drawn to the kitchen's screen door. Her husband was walking through it! I made no comment but took mental notes of his physical appearance. I was experiencing an uncomfortable feeling as my eyes were drawn to a neckpiece she wore.

"You've got to take that off," I said, pointing to the object. "Your husband won't rest until you do." I asked her what it was.

"My husband's ashes," she whimpered.

"You haven't allowed your husband to rest peacefully," I said gently. "You are causing him to remain around you. You must take his ashes and bury them. Then you'll both rest."

The tiny woman was distraught and skeptical. "Najla," she said, "I'll do what you ask if you'll come to my apartment and tell me what I want to know, without my asking you."

She was testing me but I didn't mind. "I'll do what you want," I replied. I left it to her to contact me. I realized she needed time to gather her courage. I still hadn't told her of the apparition I saw walk through the kitchen door of our friend's house. When her phone call came, I went to her home that was on the second floor of a large older house. In answer to my knock, she called down and invited me to join her upstairs. I walked up the stairs, turned right at the landing, and stopped in my tracks. She stood quietly at the head of the stairs. I said, "This is the spot where your husband died."

She rushed to me, grabbed hold of my hands and said, "I'll do what you want. You're right, he did die on that step. That's exactly what I wanted to know from you." Her husband had been a pilot on the Great Lakes for many years. I suggested she scatter his ashes on the waters of Lake Ontario. She agreed, totally convinced now of my authenticity. It was only then I gave her the description of her husband's apparition, describing his cap and sweater, height and build. She agreed that it was an exact description of him and the clothes he wore at the time of his death.

She was never troubled again by his presence. What this sad lady hadn't realized was that she had created a ghost. She had kept her husband alive by not burying his remains.

In fact, he had been an invited ghost.

* * * * * * * *

A poltergeist is another case in point of an invited spirit. This mischievous entity manifests around puberty or pre-puberty aged children, and is often confused with a spirit. A poltergeist is a field of energy that forms around a child who is confused, angry, or disturbed in some way. This negative energy collects in a child and causes phenomenal disruptions.

Pots and pans fly around the house, beds levitate, pictures fall off walls, electrical appliances turn themselves off and on, etcetera. The entire family is unhappy and usually hostile. The feelings that I experience when I enter a home with poltergeist disturbances are those of hostility. Parent against child, sibling against sibling, everyone in the house is affected. A feeling of gloom pervades the household.

I received a phone call from an anxious mother asking if I'd come to her house. She reported, "Really strange things are happening."

I replied, "You have a poltergeist. There are cupboard doors opening and closing, you're finding objects missing and they're turning up in other parts of the house."

"My God, you're right," came her startled reply. I had picked up the problem over the phone and agreed to visit the home the following day. I asked that her children be present when I visited.

When I entered her house I asked to be allowed to wander freely with no directions from the family. They were to follow me and observe. They agreed. My eyes immediately went to a massive old piano-like organ. "I don't like that," I said, "it doesn't belong in this house. Your problems began the day it was brought here."

"It belongs to my sister," the mother answered. "She

brought the harmonium with her when she moved in with us." She agreed that the occurrences had begun around that time.

I walked into the kitchen. The cupboard doors had been opening and closing, objects from them had flown around the room directed by a non-human force. The stove had turned itself off and on. I walked through the hall and up the stairs to a bedroom, the family following me. I stood at the foot of a single bed. I experienced a terrible menacing feeling! "There's a presence in this room and your daughter has seen it." I then began to absorb the destructive force.

A large floral arrangement sitting on a hope chest began to sway back and forth. This told me that I was almost ready to trap the prankish energy. The air turned very cold and the familiar feeling was inside of me. I concentrated with all my available energy on the negative force and felt the heavy feeling within me become light and the air around us turn warm.

All movement in the room stopped and I knew my work was done. I was left totally exhausted. The process had taken about twenty minutes. I've been asked if I'm not afraid that one of these negative energies might stay within me. No, I don't have that fear. Just as I am able to absorb, I am able to release. It is simply something I am able to do. Only God knows why.

A poltergeist has a life-span of about one-and-a-half years. Once a child completes puberty, the phenomena disappear. I felt that the poltergeist became active when the eleven-year-old daughter's aunt moved in with the family. It was one emotional situation too much for the girl to handle and her negative energies manifested the poltergeist.

The grateful mother called me several months later. There had been no further disturbances in the home.

Chapter 11

Kindred Spirits

I looked at the pleading woman sitting in her wheelchair. I wanted to give vent to tears. My hands were aching because she was holding them so tightly as she begged for answers. I heard her words, but my mind was elsewhere.

It was 1977 when I first met Nina. She was working in a nursing home as a registered nursing assistant. Her depths of compassion knew no bounds, nor did her energy. Her habit was to start work before her scheduled shift and to stay afterwards. She used this time to the advantage of the home's residents.

Lonely and neglected, the elderly and confined men and women relied on her benevolence to write letters or cut the toenails they could no longer reach. They especially looked forward to her soothing massages. She worked from her heart. It wasn't unusual for Nina to take residents' special clothes home to launder herself, since the commercial institutional washers weren't kind to delicates. Days off would find her transporting the recipients of her kindness to various appointments and shopping. It didn't strike me as fitting to see this virtue of kindness jailed in a wheelchair and suffering excruciating pain.

We had lost contact over the past few years. Our paths crossed again when I returned to St. Catharines after a few years absence. I was elated to hear from her when she called.

"Najla, I need to see you very badly, but I can't come to you, would you come to my house?"

"Yes, I'll come over, Nina."

She was crying as she thanked me. I was disturbed at her state of mind. This wasn't the Nina I remembered who was always bright and cheerful. Now I was here in Nina's home feeling her pain and frustration as we said our fond hellos. A paid companion was introduced to me. I followed as she wheeled her charge into the living room. I found it hard to concentrate on the present. My mind kept slipping back to all the good deeds Nina had unselfishly carried out.

I remembered the time a resident of the nursing home had mentioned to her that she had willed a diamond ring to Nina. Nina promptly refused to accept the gift. Nina had insisted that the woman had family and it should be bequeathed to one of its members. The ring had been missing and Nina, during her regular round of duties, had found it. This was a regular occurrence in the nursing home. Suffering from forgetfulness, residents would often misplace articles. Theft by the staff and other residents was also a problem. The grateful woman deferred to Nina's wish and the ring was given to a grandchild.

I was jolted out of my reverie by Nina's loud sobs. I knelt at the foot of her wheelchair and, taking her hands in mine, I asked her to tell me what had brought her to this state. Slowly calming down, she told me her unfortunate and sad story.

She had been in a car accident where her legs had been badly damaged. The original diagnosis was followed by many surgeries and a dismal prognosis. Complete recovery,

even partial recovery, was unlikely, which meant she'd probably never again have the opportunity to work and earn her
living.

Devastated, Nina prayed day and night. She wasn't willing to accept her surgeon's appraisal of her condition. She
wouldn't believe that she'd never walk again. Knowing a bit
more about medicine than the average person, Nina further
believed the proper treatment hadn't been applied to her
injured legs.

Stubbornly, she harassed her doctor into arranging a consultation with an orthopedic specialist at Chedoke Hospital
in Hamilton, Ontario. Finally, the surgeon submitted to her
demands and an appointment was made. Two years had
passed since she had suffered the car accident. Years she
had spent in and out of hospital. Years when she hadn't
walked.

The consultation with the new surgeon proved hopeful.
He didn't promise her full recovery, but after tests and x-rays
he offered a brighter picture. He felt surgery was necessary,
but she would have to be hospitalized and undergo intensive and painful therapy before he could perform it.
Overjoyed with the prospects of partial use of her legs, Nina
readily agreed to enter hospital again.

Her agonizing ordeal lasted five months. Daily she bit
her lip in pain as therapists worked with her weakened
limbs. Familiar with the effects of pain killers over a long
term, Nina would accept only minimal doses. She would
bear the pain, she told herself because it would eventually
free her from the dreaded wheelchair. She returned home to
wait for the phone call that would bring her back into hospital for the operation.

It was then that Nina contacted me. She wanted me to do
a reading for her. I was happy to oblige. Upon leaving I
asked her to keep me informed of her situation. She
promised me that she would, and asked me to pray for her. It

was with reluctance I left Nina. I wished I could do more for her. The reading had filled both of us with hope, for I picked up that she would walk again. I was also encouraged by the fact that she was blessed with a close and caring family.

Finally, the date was set for the surgery Nina hoped would restore her freedom of movement. She entered the hospital with great optimism and all went very well Her doctor gave her a prognosis she could live with— she would walk again with the use of crutches.

The second evening after the operation, Nina was very uncomfortable because of bedsores; the bane of all long-term, immobile patients. She had an ugly red rash on her derriere, and openly oozing lesions. Unable to sleep because of her discomfort, she used her call-bell to summon a nurse.

A young nursing assistant answered her call. Nina asked her to treat her badly broken skin. Gently turning her on her side, the nurse commented she knew just how to fix the wounds. She then left the room to gather the necessary materials. Her manner was very gentle, Nina thought.

Returning shortly, she attended to her patient's needs. She first bathed the red open sores with an antiseptic. The next step was to apply tape to the infected area. Having done that, the gentle attendant then placed a lambs wool square under the treated area. This was followed with placing a warm blanket over her charge.

Nina was grateful for her nurse's tender touch and the words she had soothingly spoken to her. Thanking her, Nina took her hand. Looking down on her, the nurse gently squeezed the offered hand. "You're not to worry about anything Nina, you're going to walk again." Nina asked the attentive nurse her name. "Beverly," she answered, then left the room.

Morning found Nina in a wonderful frame of mind. The discomfort she had been suffering because of her bedsores was no longer felt. She greeted the day nurse with a happy countenance.

The nurse began the routine duties involved in a bed patient's morning bath. Nina rolled onto her side to allow the bedpan to be put in place. The nurse first had to remove the tape Beverly had used on their patient. She then lifted the lambs wool square before turning Nina onto the receptacle.

Earlier, Nina's painful skin condition hadn't allowed her to stand the pressure required to sit on a bedpan. Surprised, the nurse asked Nina who had treated her bedsores. Her broken skin was completely healed over.

"Beverly," Nina answered.

"Beverly? We don't have a nurse by that name on this floor," she remarked.

"Oh, yes, she was in last night," Nina assured her. "See, she brought this lambs wool square for me too."

"I'll check your chart, and then we'll both know who treated you so successfully." The nurse leafed through the previous night's chart and shook her head.

"That's impossible, check your shift schedule. Beverly was in around 3:30 this morning. She bathed and treated my bedsores, brought me this lambs' wool square and this warm blanket," Nina insisted.

The nurse promised she'd inquire. Maybe a nurse from another floor came in, she offered. It was a puzzled-looking nurse who came back to report to Nina. She could find no request slip for either the treatment Nina had received, or the lambs wool square. There was no one by the name of Beverly working on the floor. She had checked the storage room where three allocated lambs wool squares were kept. Three were still lying on their shelf.

'There should only be two here if Nina has one,' thought the nurse. Confused, she left to check the floor below. Maybe someone from another area had nursed Nina. Her pursuit was in vain. She couldn't find the nurse Beverly, and all lambs wool squares were accounted for. It was a mystery, but a hospital is a busy place and there was little time to solve it.

Nina was released in late November and happily went home where she put the incident out of her mind. Christmas was approaching and Nina, anxious to show her appreciation and good wishes, called the hospital to ask for Nurse Beverly's address. She had sent a floral arrangement to the nursing floor staff, but she wished to send flowers directly to Beverly.

The inquiry was directed to the personnel office since information regarding her favourite nurse couldn't be obtained from the nursing station. "Beverly died about a year ago in a car accident," the voice of authority informed her over the phone.

"My God, that's why no one could find a record of her working the night she attended me!"

Nina had been compensated for her kindness to her own nursing charges by someone who obviously was tuned in to her goodness. Her deep faith in God allowed her to accept what she believed was a holy event. A relative of hers worked for the rectory of a church in Toronto and Nina, wishing to discuss the occurrence, contacted the parish priest. After hearing her story, he assured her that it hadn't been either a dream or a drug induced experience. He agreed that the tangible evidence proved otherwise.

"Najla," Nina ended her story, "I'm very fortunate to believe in God. We'd all be lost if we didn't."

"Only God could do this," I had to agree, and gave my silent thanks to Him for yet another of His many miracles.

Nina, as Beverly promised, has almost made a complete recovery. Her life has been changed, she'll never nurse again. But, she is a resilient person who studied a less demanding profession which she is enjoying today.

Nina was blessed with another visit two years after the encounter with Beverly. The recession was affecting Nina's income and she was very worried about her financial situation. While driving to work one morning she prayed for help,

as she usually does in distressed situations. Beverly suddenly appeared on the hood of her moving car. She was dressed
in her nursing uniform and smiled angelically, appearing to
be quite happy.

Nina wasn't surprised or shocked by the apparition, not
even when Beverly said, "Don't worry, everything will be all
right." After that Beverly vanished as easily as she
appeared.

Although Nina hasn't seen Beverly again, she feels her
presence around her and her home and welcomes the comfort of the angelic caregiver.

CHAPTER 12

THE GLOWING GHOST

Hamilton, Ontario, is an industrial city and the home of several steel companies It boasts a busy harbour with ocean vessels carrying steel from the Steel Capital of Canada to countries around the globe.

Barton Street, in the east end and running parallel to the many factories, is a mixture of commercial, residential and industrial dwellings. Electric buses, heavy commercial hauling rigs and workers rushing to and from the factories make it a noisy, congested part of the city. A person would never notice a particular brick house situated on Barton Street in the midst of all this hubbub. It's one of similar structures and doesn't have the appearance of the stereo-typical haunted house. Murder and mayhem would hardly come to mind if a passerby did idly happen to glance in its direction.

From 1956, when Lucille first entered the house as a three-year-old-child, until her older brother Phil was brutally beaten and murdered there in 1986, she had considered it home. I was asked to investigate after the fact.

Lucille was in a state of shock for a few years after Phil's death. She had to endure the painful and notorious trial of his sadistic murderer. Only when a verdict of guilty was pronounced could she calm down enough to contact me to tell of her traumatic association with the house on Barton Street.

"I wish to God he would have burned the house down after he killed my brother," Lucille cried as she poured out her strong emotions to me. As I watched the tears roll down her face, onto her clenched hands, it was difficult for me to hold my composure. I had read the grizzly accounts of the cruel and vicious murder without realizing it was a client's brother who was the victim.

"Why the house, Lucille," I asked. "Why would you want it burned down? What place did it have in your brother's murder?"

"It's an evil house," she answered in a resigned voice. "Tell me why you feel that way," I prodded, aware that she obviously had a great deal on her mind. Animosity towards a house is unusual without a very strong reason. I realized that she came to see me to unburden herself, not for a psychic reading. I doubted that she realized herself the intent of her scheduled visit to me. Badly in need of a compassionate ear, Lucille intuitively knew she'd find one in me. Over the years we'd established a bond of trust, and I took it as a privilege that she'd come to me in her time of sorrow and hurt.

"Tell me about the house, what happened in it that leads you to make that statement?" The hours passed as Lucille, at first haltingly and between sobs, gave her account of events that happened in her childhood home.

They started when her older sister, Sandra, left home at twenty-one years of age to start a married life. Lucille, who was now thirteen, moved into her sister's former front bedroom. Her brother Phil slept in the middle bedroom, while her parents had the back bedroom. Another sister, Gloria, was in training as a nurse at Hamilton's General Hospital and lived in residence during the week. She returned home on the week-ends.

Shortly after she moved into her new room, Lucille was awakened during the night by the sound of a howling dog. It seemed to be in the same room with her, but the family didn't own a dog. Sleepily, the teenager turned on her bedside lamp. The howling stopped, and she noticed the clock showed it was precisely 3:00 a.m. "Stupid dream," the grumpy child said to herself, before falling asleep again. She dismissed it from her mind until the next night, when she was awakened by the sound of a howling dog. Again, it seemed to be emanating from her own bedroom. Turning her bedside lamp on, she saw nothing unusual in her room. The clock, she noticed, was displaying the time at exactly 3:00 a.m. "Neighbourhood dogs," she grumbled, before falling back to sleep.

The third night, Lucille was again jarred out of a peaceful slumber to the sound of a dog howling in her room. She sat up in bed angry with the intrusion and, before she could turn her bedside lamp on, she felt she wasn't alone in the room. She saw a presence when her eyes became accustomed to the dark and felt bitterly cold. The freezing cold draft advanced from the doorway of the bedroom to her bed and it was carrying the abstract form of a man with it.

Standing at the foot of her bed, the chilling presence placed its hands on the bed and caused it to shake. Lucille was completely awake, but was overcome with fright and unable to move or speak. Hysterical paralysis had set in. After shaking the bed, the ghost left the room using the entrance he came in through. He took the cold mass of air with him. It was again 3:00 a.m.

She told her family of her frightening experience. They had all heard a dog howling during the past three nights, but paid no particular attention to a sound they commonly heard in the neighbourhood. They had adjusted to noise living on such a busy street.

Lucille, terrified to sleep in her own bedroom, started sleeping on the floor of her parents' bedroom. More than a week passed before she gathered enough courage to enter her bedroom again. She decided the only way she could sleep in that room was to totally rearrange the furniture. She never again wanted to sleep facing the door. Having done that, she moved back into her bedroom. Her parents bought her a poodle, assuring her that he could sleep with her.

Lucille's sister, Gloria, came home for her usual weekend stay from the hospital and was quickly informed of her sister's hair-raising experience. She openly laughed and criticized Lucille. How could she confuse a nightmare with reality, she chastised her young sibling. But she was happy to meet Pepe the poodle as the new addition to the family.

Around four o'clock Saturday afternoon, Gloria went into the bedroom she shared on weekends with Lucille. She asked to be awakened in an hour. About forty minutes passed before the family heard an ear-piercing scream, and saw Gloria running down the stairs.

Her parents and siblings gathered around her, asking what was wrong. Trembling and wide-eyed, Gloria told the family the cause of her upset. After calming Gloria down, the members of the family asked if what happened was caused by her imagination, resulting from Lucille's incidents. She was unshakable in her belief that someone, or something, had definitely stood at the foot of her bed. How could she imagine an indentation left on her mattress. Someone had sat on her bed! And she didn't imagine the cold draft of air that came with it.

Family members asked each other if they'd had similar, eerie experiences in the house? Philip hadn't, nor had the parents. Sandra volunteered a piece of information she hadn't earlier for fear of ridicule. Before her marriage, starting at around the time she was nineteen and for the following two years, Sandra heard nightly knocks. Knocks that emanated from her bedroom closet. She would feel a presence and hear a rapping. She never felt the cold draft or saw a presence—only a feeling of not being alone in the room.

All ghostly traffic happened in the front bedroom. They knew the previous owner's wife had died in that same room. Was she haunting it? For a while there were no further episodes to frighten the occupants of the house on Barton Street.

Lucille sat in front of the television set in the living room with her loving little poodle early one evening, when the dog suddenly began to howl—mournful, loud howls. Before she could react to her dog's unusual behaviour, he leapt from his seat beside her and headed for the stairs. Following closely behind him, she stopped dead in her tracks. There, on the staircase, stood a glowing figure! The poodle stood at the foot of the staircase and continued howling until the figure disappeared. Lucille was stunned. There was an iridescent, glowing figure. What was it? She couldn't identify it as male or female. Was it the devil she wondered? What did it want? Why did it appear and then simply dissolve as though it was vapour? Badly shaken, both the dog and Lucille sat huddled together on the chesterfield.

The next two years passed uneventfully. There was only the occasional feeling of a presence in the front bedroom, and sometimes a shadow could be seen standing at the foot of Lucille's bed. She had learned to live with these minor disturbances after the shock of the glowing ghost.

As she sat in her bedroom early one evening, she suddenly felt the spirit leave the house. She knew intuitively there would be no further paranormal experiences in her bedroom or the house. Four years later, she was married and left the home of her childhood. She had experienced no further ghostly encounters.

Now here it was, years later, and her brother had suffered a heinous death in the house on Barton Street. Both parents had died and Philip, wishing to live in the family home, bought his sisters' share of the house. The parents had stipulated in their wills that the proceeds from the sale of the home should be equally divided upon their deaths. Philip wanted to live in the house although he had never been married and lived alone. His sisters were agreeable and happy over his decision.

It would be the death of him.

Now Lucille was all talked out and had questions for me. I made a pot of tea which we took in my living room. Why was Philip killed? Why was there a ghost in her bedroom? Why did she and her dog see the glowing ghost on the stairs? Why was the world filled with such evil? Was the other side as evil? Why were there ghosts? We drank our tea, and I answered her questions by explaining the karmic laws of cause and effect.

Philip had to meet his death in such a hideous fashion because he had chosen to compensate in this lifetime for a similar deed he had perpetrated in a previous life. Ghosts come to us—not from the other side, but from this side. A ghost is a spirit who has not crossed over to another stage of spiritual development. They cling to familiar surroundings and occasionally materialize to draw attention to what they perceive as their life state. The glowing vision Lucille saw was a spirit who was trying to manifest into human form. The glow was simply the mass of energy from which all spirits are made. The spirit can manifest in different forms depending on the amount of reluctance to leave the earth plane. Some are successful in achieving almost a complete human appearance, while others who aren't so earth bound show themselves as shadowy figures, or glows. I assured her that it was all very natural and that thousands of people throughout history have seen apparitions.

As time passed, I felt Lucille begin to relax. To strengthen the statements I made to her, I gave specific examples of cases which I had personally been involved in. This seemed to comfort her.

The house was sold, Lucille and her sister Sandra were co-executrixes of their brother's estate and wanted nothing further to do with it. She asked if I could find the time to drive by the house on Barton Street to see if the people living in the home now have ghosts. She asked if I could pick that up without entering the house.

I felt there was a good chance the ghosts would again manifest in the house on Barton Street, since these were so obviously territorial spirits. "Territorial?" Lucille asked. I explained that it was the house that kept the ghosts earthbound. They coveted their territory, so to speak, and their interest was solely in the house and not its occupants. I would take a drive by I assured her.

I parked my car in a nearby lot and walked to the house on Barton Street. I wanted to view it from a vantage point across the street that allowed for a fuller view of the structure. What I observed was a black shadow covering the front and west side of the house, an indication that the house hadn't yet been released to its rightful, earthly owners.

Perhaps one day the shadow will be lifted.

CHAPTER 13

A Trilogy...Who Was Here First?

"We found another one, Najla, or it found us!" The voice on the other end of the phone belonged to Lois, a girl in her early thirties who worked as an advertising agent for a media conglomerate. Another one was a ghost, of course.

Lois and her husband Paul have shared three homes with ghostly occupants. She asked me now, "Do they find us or do we find them?" My answer was to laugh and tell her that I would be visiting their latest home and ghosts on the weekend.

I reflected back on the first home Paul and Lois had shared. It was a small story-and-a-half brick house in a non-descript neighbourhood. It was built forty-five years earlier—not your picturesque haunted house. I had been invited to dinner in their new home.

The layout was of the usual older style home: kitchen, dining room and living room on the main floor. The bedrooms and washroom were accessed from a staircase in the front entrance.

After we exchanged greeting hugs, I caught a glimpse of someone sitting on the fourth step of the staircase. To myself I said, 'Oh hello.' I didn't want to say it aloud because what I saw wasn't another dinner guest, but a ghost. I felt certain Paul and Lois had also seen this apparition of a male ghost. I didn't want to ruin their pleasure in telling me that they had seen a ghost. They were both strong believers in the paranormal and read extensively on the subject. Our conversations always included discussions on the latest books and their ideas. They kept me well informed because I'm not a reader of psychic phenomena. My tastes run to auto-biographies, historical and political novels, and two newspapers a day for stories on the world political scene. I gauged the speed at which the rest of society was accepting the evidence of life after death through this couple.

We shared a pleasant meal and made small talk about Paul's work in the building trade, Lois' latest advertising jingles and concepts, and my television show. We took our coffee in the living room and the discussion turned to ghosts.

"Najla, do you feel anything in the house?" I knew the anything they were referring to was the ghost I had seen on the stairs. I said, "Yes, there's a presence here and he lives on the fourth step of your staircase." For just a split second amazement showed on their faces. It quickly vanished to become smiles and we all laughed as they said to each other, "We should have known you'd pick it up."

Their golden retriever was whining to come in and while Paul let the dog in I said to Lois, "Your dog tipped you off about your ghost. I'm certain he'll avoid going upstairs as much as he can and when he does, he'll not touch the fourth step." She agreed on both counts. Paul joined in the conversation again and said he thought it was all very funny at first.

I asked them to tell me their story from the beginning. It

began the day they proudly took possession of their first home. They had picked up the key from the attorney's office and had gone to have a closer look at their new acquisition with their four-year-old dog. They first walked around the front and back yards before making their way to the front steps. As the couple approached the front door their dog, who had been happily running around the yard chasing the falling leaves from the shedding autumn trees, showed a reluctance to enter.

He began to pace back and forth on the porch as Lois and Paul gently coaxed him. He continued to hold back until impatience finally prompted his owners to enter without him.

The new homeowners wandered from room to room and glanced over their shoulders to see if their pet had decided to wander in on his own. He hadn't.

The satisfied couple returned to the front entrance to lock up after completing a top to bottom tour of the house. They were met by their growling, snarling dog with hind end raised high in the air and front end settled on the step framing the front door. He was staring intently at the stairs leading to the bedrooms and washroom.

Paul and Lois expressed their surprise to each other over his unusual behaviour and were unsuccessful in persuading him to calm down and move from their path. Paul used his authority over the dog, taking him by the collar and dragging him aside as his wife shut and locked the door. Once in the car with his owners the dog became his usual lovable, calm self. The happy couple put the incident out of their minds, convinced the trauma of the afternoon would not be repeated. They made moving arrangements and began packing for their first home.

The dog knew instinctively whenever they were headed to the new house, either to decorate or take packed boxes, and refused to climb in the car to accompany them. Moving day came and the dog was given little attention until the very last moment arrived and the dog had to face the new house. He did not go willingly. No amount of coaxing or treats could persuade the reluctant animal to enter the family car. Paul had no choice but to pick the large dog up in his arms and physically place him in the car. He cowered on the floor of the vehicle, not even looking up during his unhappy journey.

Paul went ahead into the house leaving Lois with the task of getting the dog out of the car. He would not budge. Exasperated with the pet and wanting to get on with unpacking and all that went with settling in a new home, Lois left the car doors open and went about her business.

Several hours later, their dog quietly entered the kitchen. The door was left open by his owners who hoped he would wander in on his own. He ate the food they left out for him, then began to wander from room to room. Lois watched him carefully, she knew he was looking for the bathroom. From the time he was tall enough to reach the toilet bowl he had refused to drink water from his bowl, preferring the water in the toilet instead. Satisfied there was no bathroom on the main floor he went down into the basement. He didn't find what he was looking for. Lois was observing his actions from the kitchen. When he approached her whining for a toilet bowl, she led the way upstairs.

He stood back and watched her head for the stairs. He didn't follow. As she began to ascend the stairs he howled in fright. 'What was it that was frightening him,' she wondered. Since he obviously wouldn't follow her lead, and realizing how thirsty he must be by the late hour of the day, Lois went into the kitchen and filled a large bowl for her seventy-pound dog. She left him sniffing dubiously at the unaccustomed, conventional bowl of water, and went upstairs to ready their bedroom for what would be a much needed night's sleep.

They completed the necessary tasks, showered, and returned to the kitchen. Their beloved dog was stretched out asleep on the floor—the water bowl was untouched. This triggered concern in both Paul and Lois. What could possibly keep their pet from going upstairs? How would he sleep downstairs alone when he had slept at the foot of their bed since they had brought him home as a pup? Lois prepared dinner while the exhausted dog slept.

Ready for bed after dinner, Paul nudged the dog awake. He gently stroked and talked to the animal, telling him that it was time for him to come to bed. The dog stumbled to his feet following his owners. They headed towards the stairs. Before reaching the foot of the stairs, the dog's ears stood straight and his fur stood on end. He snarled, growled, barked viciously, and bared his teeth. Paul and Lois looked at each other, asking, "Is he seeing something we can't?" Both were aware of the reaction animals have towards spirits and of their ability to sense or see them.

Now they felt they had the answer to the puzzle. But, how to resolve it? Too tired to give serious consideration to the situation, they felt the best course of action was no action. They walked the dog back to the kitchen, showed him his water bowl again and wished him a good night before going to bed.

The next morning began with Paul and Lois leaving for work after feeding the dog. He had left his water untouched. They released him from the house to run in the yard for the day, leaving a bowl of fresh water out for him. Paul returned home around noon to check on the dog, who was elated to see his master. The water bowl remained untouched. This upset Paul no end but he couldn't stay off work to baby-sit a confused dog.

He called the veterinarian explaining the concern he and Lois felt over the dog's refusal to drink water from a bowl and his reaction to the stairs. The doctor wasn't concerned, assuring Paul that his pet was only feeling unsettled by his new surroundings. In a day or so he would be drinking water in his usual manner. Feeling somewhat relieved Paul returned to work.

Lois came home to a very happy dog. He lovingly greeted his mistress and followed her around the house in circles. He went exploring from room to room on the main floor and down in the basement. He wouldn't go near the stairs. He seemed to have reached a decision. He would drink his water from a conventional bowl. Lois had followed him with her eyes and saw him reject the stairs again. She filled a fresh water bowl for him from which he drank in a most dejected manner. It looked like the veterinarian was right, a little time was all it would take for the dog to adjust to his new surroundings.

Nature forced the dog to break his life long habit of drinking water from a toilet bowl, but instinct stopped him from going upstairs. That same night Paul and Lois assumed their dog would now follow them upstairs to take his usual sleeping position at the foot of their bed. He didn't. He gave the same frightening performance of the previous day. Concerned, yet feeling a few more days were needed for him to overcome his personal devils, the couple bade him goodnight and went to bed. The dog reluctantly, and after some whining, returned to the kitchen to sleep for the night.

Rushing out of their bedroom and heading toward the stairs, they sleepily looked on as the dog was gingerly and bravely attempting to climb the first step. He was whining softly and looking very suspiciously at an enemy only he could see. Paul and Lois stood silently and watched him take the first step, and then another. On the third he hesitated, sensing his owners' presence he looked up and barked for them to help him. They wouldn't comply because each one wanted their dog to overcome his fear. He took the third step, jumped quickly to the fifth, turned around and fiercely

barked and growled at his enemy on the fourth step. He
flew up the remaining steps and into very welcoming arms.
Dog and masters all slept in the same bed for what was left
of the night.

The following night, as Lois and Paul prepared for bed
they called down for the dog to join them. There was no
response. Paul headed for the stairs hoping he could talk
him into following him. He lost his voice at what he saw.
Sitting on the fourth step was an apparition of an elderly
man in a hunched position, his arms loosely hanging over
his knees. A feeling of total dejection overcame him as Paul
absorbed the spirit's feelings. He softly called his wife to join
him, cautioning her with a finger to his lips to be quiet. Lois
obviously saw the ghost, and judging from her reaction Paul
could see she wasn't frightened. She was excited and
thrilled to finally see a ghost. Their own ghost!

Now that they knew the reason for the dog's terrified
reaction to the fourth step, the couple realized that their pet
would overcome his fear only by adjusting to their ghostly
guest. Paul took his wife's hand and called to his dog to
come to bed. He hesitantly approached the bottom step and
looked up silently pleading for help. As his owners beck-
oned him with their hands to join them, he began his climb.
Once he began his ascent he didn't take his eyes off the
ghost. Upon reaching the fourth step, he avoided it completely by jumping over it. The dog then turned around to
the back of the elderly spirit-man, growled and fled into the
protection of his owners' arms.

Paul and Lois remained in the house for three years, and
not once afterwards did they witness their dog touch the
fourth step. He gradually became used to his nemesis, after
a fashion. The couple knew when their ghost was present
other than at night—their dog would tell them.

He would find them wherever they were, and pull on
their clothes for them to follow him. They obliged him and

the routine was always the same. He led them to the stair-case and pointed in the direction of the fourth step. He looked up pleadingly and silently begged them to make the ghost go away. Sometimes they could see the enemy, some-times they couldn't. The couple simply accepted the ghost as another family pet.

I visited the home several times during their ownership, and on each occasion the ghost was visible to me, which caused great joy to both Paul and Lois. Very likely he is there today, since I wasn't asked to put him to rest. He will stay positioned on the fourth step until he decides to cross over, or new owners have him put to rest by an instrument similar to myself.

* * * * * *

House parties abound at Christmas time and I spend my time dodging as many as possible. I don't enjoy small talk, crowds, or the superficial. Christmas tends to expose us to all of these so I generally head for a Third World country where I can experience and share in the spiritual meaning of the holy season. Away from the commercial trappings North Americans have imposed on the celebration, I truly enjoy the genteel atmospheres of Christmases I've spent in Cuba or Mexico.

I was unable to flee this manic season in 1981 because of broadcasting commitments and found myself attending sev-eral house parties. Paul and Lois bought their second home in October and were using the occasion of Christmas to cele-brate both the season and a housewarming party.

I was looking forward to sharing in their happiness as I drove down a beautifully decorated country lane. It was Christmas card perfect, the trees covered with freshly fallen snow and the lights forming halos of colour in the descend-ing twilight that twinkled warm greetings to all road trav-ellers.

The house itself was a picture. Old, rustic, and nestled in the woods, it was a setting that would create envy in anyone wishing to live in the country. I noticed a stack of wood piled high against the closed-in side porch, and laughed to myself as I thought, 'Ah ha, they have another one.' Now I really was looking forward to a holiday house party. I was eager to hear about the couple's helpful ghost.

I didn't have long to wait. Paul greeted me at the door with a hug and said, "Naj, even you will be surprised at what we have to tell you." It was a small intimate gathering of people who knew each other well. I relaxed and enjoyed both the good food and company. There was a roaring fire in the beautiful, natural-stone fireplace, and the home showed off charming, handmade decorations that Lois had done. It couldn't have been a more authentic old-fashioned Christmas get-together. The spirit of Christmas descended upon us as we chatted gaily and drank our seasonal eggnog.

We were suddenly startled by the sight and sound of logs rolling to the floor. Paul had recently placed a pile of logs in an old-fashioned baby cradle. Now the cradle was rocking and logs were rolling. All eyes turned to me, silently asking for an explanation. *

This incident provided my hosts and guests with a truly spooky experience. Since I was certain Lois and Paul could corroborate what I'd relate, I sat back and told their ghost story.

Ghosts are as natural to meet as anyone else. I observe and make mental notes, so I can put forth both the situations created by the spirit of the deceased as well as an explanation if asked. Although I was working it didn't feel like it. The cozy atmosphere and the helpfulness of the ghost pro-

---

*   This is another reason I choose not to accept invitations to most gatherings. I'm expected to provide 'spooky' explanations for what usually turns out to be ordinary situations. Almost everybody has a ghost story they want to share.

vided me with a comfortable at home feeling.

I told my story. Yes, there was a ghost in the house. I had a captivated audience with big eyes and mouths and ears open. I told them I saw the spirit of an elderly man standing by the woodpile when I turned in the driveway. He wore a red and black plaid wool shirt, black scarf, and badly worn brown field boots. He was a large man intent on straightening the woodpile. His head and hands were bare.

I left him to his work undisturbed as I made my way to the gaily decorated front door. I wasn't in the home very long before the ghost, ignoring us all, went about his business of lovingly arranging the logs in their antique holding box. There was an air of contentment about him—he enjoyed his work. I felt that he looked on it more as a pleasure than an obligation. There was a sense of purpose about him. He left the room through the wall, as he had entered it, satisfied with what he had done.

The room was in an uproar as everyone made comments on what they saw. It was now our hosts' turn to tell their ghost story.

Within a few days of moving into their century old home they found Paul's woodpile restacked, ever so neatly. A cord of wood was delivered and since it was less expensive to stack it himself, he asked the delivery people to just leave it by the side porch. Inexperienced in the ways of stacking wood, Paul piled it haphazardly against the porch. He took some inside the porch and again piled it any which way. He did the same with the wood he placed in the baby cradle by the fireplace. He simply tossed in an armful.

The following morning Lois was the first one out of the house on her way to work. Paul noticed the neatly stacked wood in the baby cradle before leaving. 'Why would Lois, who was always running late, take time to fool around with the wood,' he thought. He left for work by the side porch.

What he saw astonished him. There, piled neatly, were

rows upon rows of fireplace wood. It was the same wood he had thrown one piece on top of the other the previous day. 'Why and how could Lois do that,' Paul wondered. He called her at work and put the question to her. She accused him of being crazy. 'Why on earth would I neatly stack a pile of wood,' she countered.

She had noticed the neat pile and thought he had done it. Since neither one of them would take credit for it, and no one else lived in their house, who had done it? When he left for work there was another surprise waiting for him. Stacked neatly against the outside of the porch was his previously messily stacked wood. It was a confused Paul who left the house that morning— convinced that Lois wasn't responsible for this surprise.

Once at work he phoned his wife to reveal to her his latest findings. She felt a friend, who simply couldn't stand the sight of improperly piled wood, may be responsible for the benevolent acts. Although she couldn't single out any one of their friends as the culprit, they accepted it as the only feasible explanation. Maybe they hadn't securely locked the door that led to the inside of the closed-in porch. They convinced each other it had to be that. They still couldn't explain the wood in the cradle, though. Together, Paul and Lois securely locked both entrance doors of the porch before retiring for the night.

The next few days passed uneventfully. The happy couple enjoyed their new home and especially the cheery warmth the fireplace provided for them. The cool evenings found husband and wife sitting contentedly chatting or reading in front of it. Missing from the cozy scene was their dog. He had developed a hip problem and been put to sleep.

It was necessary to refill the cradle towards the end of the week. Paul carelessly dropped the wood into its container, in his usual haphazard manner, leaving pieces jutting out in all directions. A neat surprise greeted them the following morning.

Again, the wood was neatly stacked in the cradle. Amazed at their find, they immediately checked doors and windows. There had to be signs of entry! 'Who was playing this practical joke,' they asked each other. All doors and windows remained securely locked. There were no signs of a physical presence, no footprints, nothing! Did one of them sleepwalk? That didn't seem likely, since one would have felt the other getting in or out of bed. Also, there was not a trace of bark anywhere. Hands touching the wood would be left rough and scratched. They checked their hands and found them smooth, clean and unscratched—and not responsible for the beautifully stacked wood.

That evening Paul installed new locks and chain locks on each of the three entry doors. The windows were then elaborately secured with nails and wooden rods that prevented them from raising. Satisfied that there was no possible way for anyone to unjam the windows or open the doors, Lois and Paul retired for the night.

Life continued as usual for the couple as they enjoyed their work and leisure time. Paul dug out his oils and began to paint again. He wanted to hang a seascape above the fireplace by Christmas. Lois kept busy and happy making decorations for the fast-approaching holiday season. They wanted to present a beautiful home to their family and friends when they came by to share in the festive season.

Again the wood-holding cradle was in need of replenishing. Paul carelessly dropped an armload into the antique receptacle. Sensitive because of the previous occurrences with the wood, Paul and Lois checked all windows and doors together. They went to bed satisfied that all locks, bolts, chains and nails were secure.

Husband and wife descended the stairs together in the morning, wanting to be mutual witnesses to what-ever sight may await them.

"We have a ghost!" Lois screeched as she gazed in

stunned amazement at a beautifully stacked pile of wood in the cradle. Paul checked doors, windows and their hands for signs that might indicate one of them had walked in their sleep and arranged the neat pile during the night. Absolutely nothing was out of place, and their hands showed no signs of roughness or scratches.

"Call Najla," Paul said to his wife. "I don't see how a ghost could be so physical, but what else can it be?" Paul wondered aloud to Lois.

"Do you suppose our ghost from the last house followed us here?" Lois asked her husband. He didn't know.

Lois phoned me that morning. Without going into detail, she asked if it was possible for a ghost to follow people from house to house. I told her it was possible but unlikely. I explained that ghosts usually attach themselves to buildings, objects, or areas. She wanted an example so I gave her one. A person who was very fond of a piano or car while living would not hesitate to play the instrument—or start up the car and turn its headlights on—or even look under the hood.

A haunted area, I explained, would be a spot where an accident happened that took the life of the now spirit. The same can hold true of a suicide site. These areas can become haunted. The spirit is trying to return to life by remaining at the location of the tragedy—in buildings that (s)he knew from a previous existence. Such a ghost is a reluctant soul, not wishing to leave a former home. Therefore it was unlikely the same spirit.

Lois gave no further information and asked no further questions other than when was I coming for a visit? I couldn't give her a specific date, due to a full calendar. She gave me the date and time of their house-warming Christmas party and asked that I make a special effort to be there. I penciled it in my appointment book. I knew I had been asked a leading question and I was eager to respond!

The accessible ghost had shown himself to me and had

now made his presence known to all the guests present. I asked Paul and Lois to tell us their ghost story from the very beginning.

Their spellbound audience listened intently as each of our hosts shared in telling the story. They answered all their guests' questions before turning to me to ask, "Najla, what should we do, should we keep him, or send him on his way?" I said I felt it was their decision. If they wanted me to put him to rest, I would. If they wanted to keep him around as a conversation piece, for company, or out of simple curiosity, that was also their decision.

I understood the excitement the ghost had generated in their lives. I also knew they had developed an affection for their helpful ghost. However, knowing that every ghost is created from a very personal and severe inner conflict, I suggested that they consider the root-cause of their ghost. I gently pointed out that if a friend was suffering, would they not offer their help to ease the situation? Thoughtfully, they looked at each other. Their conscience, I knew, wouldn't allow them to keep their ghost. I saw them very reluctantly draw to a conclusion.

I stood to leave, as this wasn't an appropriate occasion at which to conduct an exorcism. My presence now would only cause all present to feel uncomfortable. What had begun as a cheery gathering was now a serious situation, and only my leaving would allow the party to carry on. I said good-night to everyone, leaving Paul and Lois standing at their gaily decorated front door smiling uncertainly as I drove off.

I left for a holiday in January and returned to find a message from Paul to call. I returned his call a few days later. We chatted about Christmas, New Year's parties, and my holiday before he started discussing the subject that prompted his call—their ghost. Since we had last seen each other more than three weeks had passed—three weeks during which the ritual of straightening Paul's carelessly piled wood continued.

Another cord of wood was delivered in the first week of January. Lois and Paul stacked it in the closed-in side porch. They told each other it looked quite neat. Each then carried an armful and placed it neatly in the cradle-woodbox. They then enjoyed the fruits of their labour by relaxing in front of the lovely glowing fire. They fell asleep in front of the fire, deeply contented.

They were awakened a short while later. Slowly, as sleep faded and wakefulness took over, they saw what had caused them to wake from their unscheduled and cozy sleep. The wood in the cradle had been re-arranged again. They couldn't see the ghost, but they could feel his presence in the room. Slowly, they walked to the door opening into their side porch. Here too the wood was neatly stacked. They didn't like it. What kind of a life was that for a ghost, they asked each other. Forever stacking wood wasn't something they wished on anyone, living or dead. Paul now wanted me to put the ghost with a mission to rest. I would comply.

There was very little for me to do when I arrived again at their lovely century-old home. It was a somber couple who greeted me at the front door. Both had developed an empathy towards their compulsive ghost.

"I feel sad and sorry to see him go, but I'd feel sad and sorry if he had to stay," Lois softly said. I understood their emotions. This wasn't an average couple. An unshakable belief in the spirit world made them sensitive to the feelings of others, including ghosts. We all desire a restful afterlife, and here was an opportunity to provide just that for the spirit who was lost in time. The feeling of comradeship was strong among us.

I asked them to stay a slight distance behind me as I walked towards the living room. I picked up only a slight presence as I approached the fireplace. Standing in front of it, I gently willed the woodstacker's spirit to rest. I could sense his willingness to find his peace as I did. I spent perhaps three minutes concentrating in the area before moving on into the side porch.

Here the spirit had been a little busier and there was more of him to pick up. I directed my energies on both the inside and outside of the porch, since he had been in both areas. I couldn't see him, but I could feel his presence. I raised my arms and silently spoke with him, encouraging him to go to his rest. I extended the heartfelt concern Paul and Lois expressed for his well being and bade him go. I could feel him leave quietly and peacefully.

Paul and Lois remained in the house for four years after the ghost was put to rest. During that time there was no sense of a presence, nor were the sloppy woodpiles tampered with. Their helpful ghost had crossed into his own dimension.

* * * * * *

"Another house, another ghost, Najla," Lois informed me when we met briefly while shopping. "I don't like this, it feels menacing. Will you pay us a working visit?" I agreed to drop in late that Saturday afternoon, since Paul and Lois were habitually late risers on week-ends.

I was greeted on my arrival by their recently acquired dog. This one was a lovable mongrel. The older home sat on a large lot and was badly in need of maintenance. A barn that hadn't been used in what appeared to be centuries leaned precariously to one side, its roof partly missing because of rot.

'Good grief, what have they done,' I thought, as I took in the none-too-attractive view. I walked around the lot before entering the house to see if I could pick anything up. The dog followed me, yapping playfully at my heels. I entered the house through the front door, feeling nothing unusual in the way of a presence. Lois, who was waiting for me in the back kitchen, called me in.

I stopped in the entrance doorway and looked straight ahead to a staircase. I shuddered. I saw an elderly woman in a most emaciated condition. She was standing on the stairs and seemed to be trying to say something. Concentrating further, I realized that she wasn't trying to talk; she was choking. She had been murdered!

"You've seen her, haven't you?" Lois asked. I then realized that she had purposely not met me at the door. She had stayed out of my view to be able to judge my reaction upon entering. I nodded yes, and shuddered again before walking away.

Seated at the kitchen table drinking tea, I asked Lois what prompted them to buy a house that was so obviously in need of repair. She explained they bought it on speculation that the lot could be severed, assuring them of a substantial return from their investment. They had a dream house in mind and this seemed to be a quick way of acquiring it.

"Now, let's talk about the ghost," I said. "She was murdered," I added, "but before she was, she was badly mistreated."

"When you feel you have the energy to face the stairs again, I want to take you up to the attic," Lois answered.

My stomach knotted. I knew I'd be upset at what I'd pick up. I took my time drinking the tea, lingering over the second cup. Lois, noticing my hesitation commented, "You're already picking it up, am I right?" I replied that I was, and proceeded to relay to her my impressions of events which had led to the sorrowful, pitiful ghost.

"I feel a young man in his mid-thirties, tall, thin, dark hair and beard, dressed in clothing I judge would be worn at the turn of the century. He seems to be carrying food upstairs—to the elderly lady I saw on the stairs as I entered."

Having entered the state I needed, I made my way to the front staircase with Lois following. I felt compelled to go up into the attic. I felt the tired old soul on the stairs as I headed to the attic. We entered a partially finished and furnished sitting room. An old straw-stuffed chesterfield, a small end table with candles and holder sitting on it, a small chest of drawers, a few wooden crates and boxes made up the contents of the oppressive room.

"Lois, the old woman was kept in this room by the young man, who I feel was a relative. She had to take her meals here. She was confined to this room! I feel like I'm choking." I wanted to return downstairs. I knew all I wanted to know. I'd try to put the tortured soul to rest from the bottom of the stairs.

We sat in the living-room for a short time, as I needed to restore my energy. We passed a few moments in silent contemplation before I said, "Lois, I fully believe the woman was hung in the upstairs attic room."

"We made inquiries in the area after we encountered the woman you saw on the stairs," she volunteered. It seems her young nephew lived in the house with her. He cared for the house, the animals and the land. His elderly aunt died in the upstairs room under mysterious circumstances. We haven't been able to find anyone who could lead us to a complete, accurate account."

I was frustrated by the fact that what I picked up couldn't be corroborated, however that wasn't as important as putting the spirit to rest.

I faced the staircase, summoned the energy I needed and began the absorption process. Raising my arms to allow the energy to move through me, I willed the spirit to its rest. I felt heavy and oppressed as I did so. Chilled to the bone, and with my throat constricting, I stood firm as I willed and anticipated the spirit's release.

It came slowly inch by inch, traveling from my toes up through my body and to the tips of my fingers. I felt her leave her ghostly imprisonment. I had absorbed her and released her.

Lois and I stretched out on the living room sofas exhausted, where Paul found us on his return home. "By the looks of you girls I'd say you've seen a ghost," he quipped.

Smiling weakly I replied, "Smart aleck, don't you ever dare to buy a house without asking me first." We all laughed, but I was serious. I asked about their dog and how he handled the ghost?

"Oh, he won't go upstairs," Paul replied.

"Bring him in, I want to see if he will now," I asked Paul.

The dog took no coaxing to enter the house and ran around the living room licking us all. Paul stood up and called to his dog to follow up the stairs. At first he hung back. Then slowly, as Paul gently called him to his side, the dog apprehensively ventured towards his master and the stairs. Paul sat on the bottom step and motioned for his pet to come to him. He took a few minutes to decide, then slowly he made his way to Paul.

Paul started up the stairs. After a brief period of analyzing the situation, the dog trotted up behind his master and right up into the attic sitting room. Lois and I quietly awaited their return. Down they came, dog and master, nonchalantly walking past us and out into the kitchen. Paul was anxious to give his animal a treat and happy to make a fresh pot of tea for Lois and I.

CHAPTER 14

STOP, THIEF!

A ghost will sometimes steal to make a statement. How often have you looked in one particular spot for a missing article, only to have it turn up in that exact spot later? You're not alone.

Ursula had placed a heavy gold chain in her jewellery box. She was sure she had, but when she went to wear it the chain wasn't there. She asked her husband Henry if he had seen the chain. He hadn't. 'Why would he go into her jewellery box,' he asked annoyed. She had been away for the weekend and during her absence he had vacuumed. She thought the box might have been accidentally tipped over when he moved the dresser. He helped her to look for it. Nothing.

Ursula mentioned that several weeks earlier while she was lying in bed one night, a cold chill crept up her body just as she was falling asleep. It started at her toes and worked its way up. She said she felt that something was there.

What she had described was a ghostly presence. There was something there. A mischievous presence is always accompanied by a cold chill. I told her that I felt she had experienced a visitor from the other side and most likely it would return. Her father had recently died, leaving Ursula and her brother disputing the sale of a piece of property. It had been handled in such a way by her brother that Ursula was left with a very small part. The injustice of it had created an understandable rift between the two siblings.

I was familiar with her family background and told her that I felt her father had paid her a ghostly visit. This only added to her discomfort. First his death, then the betrayal by her brother, and now a haunting!

I calmly assured her there was a good reason for his visit and it would be shown to her shortly.

Ursula and Henry spent four days in a row looking for the gold chain. Opening the jewellery box and dumping its' contents on the bed did not produce the chain. On the fifth day, Ursula reached into her jewel box for a piece of jewellery. There lay the missing gold chain! A chill ran up her spine as my words came back to her.

The chain had belonged to her deceased mother. Ursula had been given the fourth generation heirloom when she died—at least part of it. A gold watch was meant to hang from the chain. The watch was given to her by her father. When she asked for the matching chain he argued he wanted to give it to a cousin. The rest of the family disagreed, confronted their father, and the chain was given to Ursula.

Replacing the chain after taking it was her father's way of apologizing to Ursula for the bad feelings his deed had created. He had to first draw her attention by taking the chain before he could give her this message. Being a ghost can be just as frustrating as being human.

* * * * * *

The following story was related to me by a friend.

"My son's soft leather baby bootie wasn't in his crib

when I went in his room to pick him up from an afternoon nap. Where could a four-month-old put a bootie? I looked all over his crib moving and picking up blankets. The bootie had disappeared! I settled Bruce in his playpen and went back into his room to look for the bootie. I moved his crib away from the wall when I didn't find it, thinking it had been jammed between the wall and crib. It wasn't there.

"Next, I removed all the blankets from the mattress and shook them. Nothing fell out. I then lifted the mattress out of the crib. Now the entire crib and the floor beneath it was exposed. No bootie. Since I had his crib apart, I decided it was a good time to give it a scrubbing.

"I washed the crib rail by rail. I then wiped the plastic mattress and metal springs. I put the clean crib back against the wall. There was no soft leather baby bootie in the crib or in Bruce's room. I bought my son a new pair of booties and tried to put the incident out of my mind, yet it seemed so strange. It was much stranger when I discovered his little lost bootie two months later when I was putting my son down in his crib for the night! We had been told by neighbours that the house was haunted, but we were skeptical. Now, we believe it."

CHAPTER 15

DANCING THE Night Away

"He was dancing, whistling and wearing white spats over black patent leather shoes." He was a spirit.

Trudy sat across the table from me in her cozy kitchen. She had a defiant look in her eyes, almost daring me to disbelieve her. I had been concerned about her for almost three weeks. We were close friends and spoke on the phone several times a week and saw each other often.

She had been house-sitting for her niece over a long weekend, and had been acting strangely ever since. My calls to her weren't returned nor did she stop by to visit. She phoned mid-morning and asked me to come over, saying that she needed to talk. She sounded so subdued it bothered me. "Najla, I consider you to be my best friend, but I couldn't confide this to even you, till now."

By nature Trudy is easy-going and fun-loving. She has never had a problem expressing herself and her vocation puts her on public display. Trudy is a history teacher and is loved for her teaching talents. I looked at my friend and felt her confusion. I said nothing as I waited for her to continue with her story.

"Najla, I saw a ghost from the past and he looked like he was performing in an old Fred Astaire movie." It was obvious Trudy was reliving an experience that she couldn't quite grasp. I only nodded, waiting for her to continue. My silence encouraged her to do so.

"He wasn't a large man, slight of build, in fact. I was stretched out on the couch in the den reading when my eye caught a movement on the stairs leading to the upstairs bedrooms. I half glanced in the direction of the stairs, and I think I stopped breathing. He was watching me, and I felt he had been waiting for me to notice him." I continued to listen quietly and this had the effect I hoped it would. She was gaining confidence and continued with her account of the debonair spirit.

"When our eyes met he immediately began to step dance on the stairs. Then he was whistling, I don't know what tune he was whistling, but he was enjoying himself and my company."

Trudy looked at me and said, "I know I don't have to ask you to believe me, I know you do. But you have to realize how shocking this is to me. I was looking forward to a peaceful weekend by the lake, and I could have been a dance partner to a ghost!"

I couldn't contain my laughter, it exploded from me and Trudy suddenly was laughing with me. We laughed till we cried and continued even after we dried our eyes. I reminded Trudy that every drama, given the proper amount time, will have its own humor.

"Time, Najla, that's what I needed—to spend time with myself and reflect on what I saw and felt." I appreciated and respected her intelligent approach to an abnormal situation.

"I thought your work was so exciting," she said, looking

pensively at me. "But I can see now it isn't. It's quite serious." My friend had truly gone inward while in seclusion
and had fortunately come out of it much wiser.

She was ready to continue. "Suddenly, he was gone. In
front of my eyes, he vanished. Gone, just like that," she said,
snapping her fingers. "When my niece and her family
arrived home, I didn't mention the incident to them. I found I
couldn't talk about it. I didn't want to. Now I can discuss it
with you, Najla, why did I see a ghost?"

Trudy felt she had been intruded upon, and she had. But
the spirit didn't feel the same. To him, she was in his territory. "Trudy, I'm willing to bet a trip to Mexico you're not the
only person to see this man's act in that house. Why don't we
ask your niece if any of her family has seen the entertaining
ghost."

"I think I'm ready to do that now," Trudy agreed. I felt
she was drained of energy and I should take my leave. We
hugged good-bye and I reminded her that I was expecting
to hear from her when a time for our visit had been
arranged.

A few days later I was back.

"Oh, you saw Oscar." said Trudy's niece, Fran.

"What do you mean, I saw Oscar?" Trudy almost exploded. "You knew you had a ghost and you let me stay here
alone, without telling me?" Trudy demanded. "How could
you?"

Fran's laughter wasn't doing Trudy's temper any good.
She was fanning the fire. Turning to me Trudy said, "Can
you believe this, I do them a favour and they spring a ghost
on me?" Now I was laughing. Trudy's indignation seemed
inappropriate, the spirit had been entertaining her after all.

I spoke my thoughts and Trudy finally saw the humor in
the situation. Her smile became a laugh, a good, healthy,
cheerful from the bottom of the stomach laugh. "Let me
walk through the house," I said to Fran. "I want to investi-

gate this spirited spirit."

She was only too happy to allow my request.

The house was built at the turn of the century and stands atop an embankment sloping onto Lake Ontario. It's a comfortable looking house with a verandah around the entire front. The view was spectacular. Toronto is to the North while Lewiston, New York is to the south. A rose garden circles the entire property.

'What a magnificent painting this would make,' I thought. I nudged myself out of my reverie and went back to the main entrance. Letting myself in, I walked up the same stairs the spirit had used to entertain Trudy. 'Just as I thought, a territorial spirit,' I said to myself when I saw him. He danced his routine for me, smiled, turned his back and walked away. "Wow, are you ever letting me know I'm in your space," I said aloud.

I continued on up the stairs, walking from room to room, I could sense no other spirits. 'Oscar,' as Fran's family called him, was their only inhabitant from the other side. I found Fran and Trudy sitting in the den.

"Well, I've swept the house for ghosts, and I can't find any. Other than your Oscar that is. I've a question for you, Fran. Why was he named Oscar?" I was certain that I knew the answer, but I always ask for verification of my feelings and thoughts.

"I was the first one to see him," Fran explained. "I was sitting where Trudy was when she saw him. I was startled, yes, but I wasn't frightened. I didn't feel threatened in anyway. Oscar just came to mind. I can't say why."

"He wanted you to call him by his proper name," I said, "and using telepathy, he conveyed that message to you," I explained.

"How do you know that?" Fran asked.

"He has a healthy ego, I believe he performed on the stage while living, and is now busily reliving his glory days."

"Once a ham, always a ham?" Trudy asked.

"Basically, yes. Your Oscar is lost in time. He's reluctant to release what he feels is his only security, and that's his talent. He's earthbound because he's convinced himself that he's still a performer, and having an audience provides him with the energy he needs to hang around.

"Do you mean to say that if we ignored him during his display of talent he would leave?" Fran asked.

"Yes, it's as simple as that," I answered. "Without an audience he has no desire to perform."

"My God," Trudy exclaimed, "don't men ever lose their egos? They actually take it with them, is that what you're saying, Najla?"

"Some do. Don't forget, every spirit has a personality, and especially those who manifest," I reminded them. "It isn't the spirit that dies, only the body. Trudy, you attended the lecture when I spoke on this subject," I reminded her.

"Yes, I remember, and like everyone else, I was fascinated by what you said," she answered. "And I believed what you were saying. But, when I was confronted with a dancing and whistling ghost, he wasn't a spirit. To me, he was a real man who had returned from the dead, and it frightened me."

"Of course you were frightened." I assured her this was quite normal. I turned to Fran, "It's up to you and your family, if you want Oscar to entertain you, he'll stay, if you ignore him when he performs, he'll leave," I said. "It's as simple as that," I promised her. "Take away his reason for living and he'll be gone."

Fran discussed my visit with her husband and two children and they agreed to ignore the flamboyant performer in the future. It worked very well. Oscar hasn't been seen or heard from in several years.

CHAPTER 16

THE PREGNANT GHOST

I must admit that I was hesitant to include this story of the haunted mother-to-be. Pregnancy, under normal circumstances, is a joyous time of expectation. However, this wasn't to be for Evelyn. Her experiences left me feeling quite sad even after I put an end to the horrendous deeds created by the cruel entity that entered her life.

I assume the reason this case still holds sadness for me is that it was my first experience with what most would term the Devil.

I met Evelyn, a twenty-six-year-old lab technician, when I visited friends in their new condominium in Kitchener, Ontario. Matt, Gloria and I were enjoying a cup of coffee and pleasant conversation when we were interrupted by a knock on the door. A woman in the advanced stages of pregnancy was ushered into the living room. She had obviously been crying for some time. Her swollen, red eyes attested to that.

She hesitated when she realized Gloria and Matt had company. I stood to shake her hand when Matt made the introductions. I turned ice cold when I took her extended hand, and then felt a strong urge to protect her. She joined us for coffee. As we chatted I felt very sorry for her state of discomfort. She tried to be specific in our conversation, but her mind wandered. We asked the usual questions one does when in the presence of a mom-to-be: when she was due, did she want a boy or a girl, how was her husband enjoying the anticipation? She seemed to have trouble answering. She was quite hesitant. Suddenly, she stood up, apologized for disturbing us and left.

I asked a startled Matt and Gloria if they had told Evelyn they had a psychic friend. I thought perhaps my name might have been mentioned and she felt uncomfortable around me. I was certain that wasn't it because of what I had picked up from Evelyn, yet I had to ask the question. They assured me that they hadn't discussed me or psychic phenomena with her. This was only her third visit to their condo and they hadn't yet met Eric, her husband. I was gravely concerned for the well-being of Evelyn and her baby. That concern proved to be well-founded and was to take me back to Kitchener several times.

Before leaving for home, I expressed my concern to my friends and asked them to contact me if Evelyn needed me. They didn't ask questions and promised to do as I asked. Three days later I received a call from a troubled Gloria. Evelyn was with her and they both wanted to talk to me. Gloria explained she had seen some astonishingly strange things in what was to be the baby's nursery. Confronted with visual proof of a haunting, Gloria told Evelyn of the work I do and suggested she call me. When the women told me what they had seen and experienced, I wasn't surprised. The ice cold chill I experienced when I met Evelyn told me there was an angry spirit with her. I didn't, however, know just how angry.

Since I would not be able to get to Kitchener for another four days, I asked Evelyn to call her priest, explain to him what had happened and ask him to visit and bless the home and family. She agreed to do this. "Najla, you won't believe this, you just won't believe this," Evelyn kept repeating.

"Calm down, please, let's have a coffee," I told Gloria upon my arrival at her home. After our coffee, I led Gloria into a calming state of meditation. When I felt she was suitably relaxed, I asked her to share her ghostly experience with me.

It was ghastly. Evelyn was four weeks from delivering her baby and for the past month she had been plagued by uncanny events and they were becoming more bizarre as the due date drew closer.

Evelyn had indeed been crying when I met her. Not understanding what was happening, she had confided in no one but her husband Eric, who worked a steady four to twelve shift at a local factory and wasn't at home when the confounding events happened. He tried to convince his wife there had to be a rational explanation for what she had described to him.

There had been an occurrence at the time of my visit, and nerves stretched taut by the seemingly unending disturbances, Evelyn fled her condo in search of comfort and help. She had been taken aback by the presence of a stranger when she entered her neighbours' home, and feeling ashamed, she had left soon after her arrival. She was back in a few days, however, and this time she stayed and asked for help. Believing in the paranormal and experiencing it are two absolutely different things. Gloria and Matt believed in psychic phenomena but had never personally seen it. They were about to. Gently they calmed Evelyn and asked her to tell them what frightened her so.

It had begun when she was in her seventh month, she said. She noticed objects missing from the nursery—pictures on the wall, little nighties and blankets. The objects were always returned in a few hours and always placed in the expected baby's crib. Evelyn could also hear the light being switched on and off in the nursery, sometimes even when she was in it. Eventually, she became convinced she had a ghost.

The day I met her, she had heard sounds coming from the prepared nursery and, upon investigating, was faced with a horrible scene. The crib blankets had been shredded and strewn throughout the room. She couldn't fight back the nausea and tears. Finally, in desperation she had knocked on her new neighbours' door, only to leave feeling totally helpless.

When her husband arrived home from work and saw the shredded and strewn blankets, he was convinced something unnatural was happening in his home, and more specifically, around his unborn baby. After this incident, bizarre events happened on a more frequent basis. It was during such an event that Evelyn ran from her condo to Gloria's and told her story, begging for help. A stunned Gloria listened and eventually agreed to go back to Evelyn's with her to view the wrath of the unseen visitor.

What a sight it was! Furniture had been moved, drawers opened and their contents spilled out on the floor, and again, shredded blankets. It was hard to believe no human had created the horrendous mess.

"Najla, do you believe me?" a frightened Gloria asked. I assured her that I did and asked to be taken to Evelyn and Eric, who were expecting me.

"It wants your baby," I said as I stood in the nursery. Everyone gasped loudly. "There's an evil force in this room and it's waiting to possess your newborn baby," I said. Even to my ears this sounded unbelievable, but I felt certain the baby, once born, would be in danger.

I explained what I felt in the room. The coldness, the terribly cold air we could all feel, but I could also feel and smell evil. The entity had a sense of control about it, I explained, and I knew I could do nothing to help until close to the time of birth.

I felt both an emptiness and heaviness as we all left for Matt and Gloria's house. I asked for the priest's reaction to Evelyn's story. She felt he didn't quite believe her. He had blessed the home and asked Evelyn to have faith and pray. Good advice, but I knew it would take more than that. I had a theory and wanted to test it on Evelyn.

"Evelyn," I began, "I think you're the spirit."

"What?" Tears and shock sprang to her eyes.

"Yes," I continued, "I believe you have somehow invited the spirit into your home." I sat beside her, took her hand and gently explained the many different types of spirits. As they listened, I explained my shocking observations. The most dangerous and possessive spirit is one who's waiting on the other side for an opportunity to manifest. They want to live because they aren't satisfied to be a ghost and simply hang out. They wait for an opportunity to inhabit the body of a living person.

However, to do this they must be invited. "Have you been using a Ouija Board?" I asked. She shrank back into the sofa, released my hand, covered her mouth and nodded her head yes.

"My cousin brought one over one night. We were curious to know if I was having a boy or girl. We placed our hands on the little table, asked the question and it began to move slowly around the board, stopping on the letter M, then it went to the letter I, circled the board a few times before it stopped on the letter N, then went directly to E. It wouldn't move after that. What does it all mean?" Evelyn asked.

"It means," I explained, "that you invited a spirit into your body at that moment. It's waiting to possess the baby once it is born." We were all badly unnerved by the horrendous situation. I asked if the Ouija Board incident coincided with the onset of the disturbances.

"Come to think of it, they did. I walked down the hall to the bathroom and passed the nursery when my cousin left. I noticed the light was on. It wasn't earlier, I was sure." Evelyn said.

I asked Evelyn and Eric to call their priest and ask for an exorcism. The couple was terrified, and I certainly was in no way calm. I was quite frightened for them. Gloria and Matt asked if there was something I could do. I hadn't at that point in my career dealt with such an evil force and wasn't even certain that I could. They agreed to call the family priest. I asked to be kept abreast of any developments. They promised to keep me informed.

One week later, I received a phone call from Eric. Evelyn was sleeping and he was consumed with worry and frustration. The priest had paid the couple a visit, listened to their story, consoled and prayed for them. But an exorcism, he explained, would take a good deal of time to arrange. The Church hierarchy would have to be petitioned for such a service to be conducted. It couldn't be done within the short time remaining before the baby's arrival. He did promise to spend some time every evening with Evelyn while Eric was working. "We'll have to be satisfied with that," I consoled Eric. "It will help, I'm sure."

It didn't. Father Timothy and Evelyn were chatting in the living room one evening the following week, when suddenly there was an ear splitting crash from the nursery. Rushing into the room, they saw the lamp on the dresser had been knocked over with such a force that it took everything from the top of the dresser with it upon falling. This wasn't an accident, the priest stated. A very frightened and yet relieved Evelyn collapsed, and Father Timothy quickly and gently brought her around.

Leading her out of the room, he never stopped praying. I

was called early the next morning with the news. "The spirit was angry that the priest was in the home and expressed it in a most dramatic fashion," I said. "Eric, I feel your wife will go into labour this afternoon, don't leave her alone for even one second."

I asked for the priest's phone number and told Eric I'd be in Kitchener by early evening. He was to leave the key to the condo with Matt and Gloria. I would try to exorcise the evil spirit out of the house before the baby was born. I called Father Timothy and begged for his help. I explained what I wished to do and asked him to meet me. He was very compassionate and complied.

Before leaving for Kitchener, I entered a deep state of meditation for about twenty minutes and found the strength and courage I was seeking. I was now on my way to confront the devil.

Father Timothy was at Matt and Gloria's when I arrived. I asked the frightened couple for the key to their neighbours' condo. I took it, then handed it to Father Timothy, asking him to bless it. He carried a black satchel from which he withdrew a rosary and gold cross, handing them to me, he asked that I wear them. He then blessed us both with holy water. Taking his satchel with him, we left for Evelyn's and Eric's house.

Immediately upon entering the condo, the somber priest withdrew a large crucifix and a prayer book. He placed a white and gold embroidered cloth over his shoulders and motioned to me to follow him. While Father Timothy was fearful and anxious to rid the evil inhabiting the family's home, I was strangely calm. Strength and courage were with me and I believed we would be successful in our mission.

We weren't prepared for the startling sight that met our eyes. We stood in the doorway of the nursery in total shock and amazement. Hovering above the centre of the baby crib was a red ball of what appeared to be fire.

Father Timothy took my hand and began to pray. We walked to the crib and I began to talk to the evil mass hovering and dancing not one foot away from us. I willed it, in the name of God, to leave. I reminded it that it was dead and had been on its way to Bardo. It was meant to continue on its way. I assured the entity there would be another life and that he only had to return to the other side, review his past lives and choose a new one to again be back on earth in human form. Father Timothy didn't stop praying while I spoke. We each continued our mission, holding hands and shivering because it was unbelievably cold in the room. The cold emanating from the red ball of fire was definitely below freezing temperature.

We weren't aware of the passing of time and didn't realize until afterwards that we had been with the spirit for almost two hours. It would begin to diminish only to burst back into a brighter light. Ultimately, it began to hiss and consistently lose color. Finally, at long last, it vanished. Warmth returned to the room and with it a sense of peace and calm.

Father Timothy and I continued our prayers for some time. He led me in the conventional and familiar prayers of the Rosary. Matt and Gloria had spent their time in prayer waiting for us and expressed great relief at our return. There was no need to tell them that we had been successful, they both said it showed. They could sense our calmness.

We needed to notify the expectant parents to complete our mission. I called them at the hospital to give them the joyous news. He was on his way to join them and wait out the arrival of the baby. He didn't have long to wait. Within the half hour Evelyn delivered a healthy and beautiful daughter. Many years have passed, and the family in the ensuing years hasn't suffered further visitors from the other side.

This story is a classic example of the reasons I'm opposed

to seances or efforts to contact the dead. There are evil spirits waiting for an opportunity to possess a living person, and while there have been successful and peaceful attempts to contact the other side, it's far too risky, and I believe shouldn't be tried.

CHAPTER 17

MOTHER LOVES ME NOW

Tears, tears, and more tears.

They poured out of Norma.

She was badly in need of this catharsis. I silently sat across the room from her while the healing process was running its course. It had taken us eight years to reach this moment of release. More than forty years of pain, suffering and torment were now being put to rest. It had taken me less than one hour to put Norma's long years of emotional trauma to rest.

Thus ending her possession.

Hilda, Norma's mother, was a psychopath. The dictionary defines such a person as one who exhibits amoral and anti-social behaviour. The pain and anguish of being raised by such a person can only be described as horrendous.

There is some good in everyone and it was to this part of

Hilda's character that I directed my appeal. Successfully, as I knew I would be when I arrived at my friend Lucille's home, where Norma was to meet me.

A mountain of snow was poised on either side of the driveway. I looked at one mound, then the other. I couldn't believe Lucille had shoveled her double size driveway herself. We had suffered through seven snow storms this season and the last one had been brutal, with high winds making it almost impossible to keep roads, walks and driveways cleared. We had spoken earlier in the week to verify the scheduled meeting for this Saturday. Lucille had mentioned during our conversation that she had been forced to take a day off work due to straining her back from shoveling the ice encrusted snow covering her driveway. 'I'll have to do something about her back before I leave,' I said to myself.

First, a much more serious mission awaited me. I was about to do something I had wanted to do for the past year. I was very much looking forward to my task.

Lucille and Norma had been close friends from the time of their teen years. In the ensuing twenty-nine years, each had married, raised children, developed careers, and kept close contact. Shortly after I met Lucille, she mentioned her friend to me, expressing concern for her well being. "The poor soul will have no peace until after her mother dies," was my prophetic comment.

It was several years later that Norma came to me for a psychic reading. During her reading I gave a complete description of her life, beginning with her earliest years.

It had been a particularly unhappy life. One of emotional abandonment, physical neglect and an absence of motherly love.

Her mother's psychopathic nature precluded feelings of love, concern, compassion and responsibility. Norma listened intently as I spoke. Upon completion of my reading she had one question for me.

"Why, Najla? How could I be born to such an evil woman?"

"Reincarnation, you have chosen this Karma," I explained.

"Would you do a reincarnation reading for me, Najla? I have to find out why I chose to do this to myself," Norma said.

"Of course," I'd be happy to help you find the answers," I assured her.

Norma's past lives reading went very well; in that it provided her with the answers to that monumental and all encompassing question—why?

I handed her the taped account of the reading, asking her to listen to it any time she felt depressed or was going through a difficult period in her life. The answers she sought were there.

Difficult though it may be to accept that we are, in fact, the masters of our fate, the engineers of our life structure and the executioners of our destiny. Once we realize this it allows us the gift of acceptance. Accepting our Karma releases a flow of freedom—freedom from fear, anger, anxiety and regrets. But what of a possession beyond the grave? This is what Norma's mother had in mind for her.

We had remained in touch socially after Norma's reincarnation reading, sharing evenings of dinner and concerts where I met her husband and children. She seemed to be happy and in control of her life.

Then her mother died.

The psychopath's main objective in life is control. They must manipulate all those with whom they come into contact—be it children, co-workers, or authority figures of any type.

The past life reading provided Norma with her reasons for choosing Hilda as her mother. It had not, however, prepared her for her mother's after death possession. Hilda, consumed with her lust for control, entered her daughter's physical body after she died— thus Norma had in fact become her own mother.

I had anticipated this occurrence at the time of Norma's psychic reading. I wasn't surprised therefore, to receive a phone call from an anguished Lucille concerning Norma's state of mind and body.

"I'm so worried about her, Najla, I don't know what to do. How can I help her?"

"She's getting worse by the day it seems. She wants a divorce, she's stopped working, and she's very sick, physically and emotionally. Her doctor has given her two years to live. I don't understand it, suddenly, she's gotten old, and I don't even know her any more."

"Lucille, can you have her at your place this Saturday morning? Tell her I'd like to see her. I have a theory and I don't think I'm wrong."

Lucille agreed to call her and extend the invitation. Reluctantly, Norma consented to my request.

I had specifically asked for the meeting to be held at Lucille's home because I felt it would be neutral territory. In other words, Hilda would have no interest in haunting Lucille or her residence. Therefore, my job would be that much easier.

Had I chosen to enter Norma's home and attempt the exorcism there, with Hilda in residence so to speak, my task would be considerably more difficult.

I would have to rid the house of Hilda's spirit first, then exorcise her from Norma's body. I was going to apply my favourite theory, KISS—keep it simple stupid—by having Norma meet me at Lucille's.

By removing Norma from her home for the exorcism, I would only have to perform the act once, being that Hilda was with Norma and I would be able to remove her from Norma's residence while I ended the physical possession of her daughter.

A beleaguered looking Lucille opened the door to my knock. Her neck was hunched down into her shoulders in pain. 'I really have to fix that for her before I leave,' I thought as we hugged hello.

When Norma arrived I was not at all surprised at her appearance. One did not have to be psychic to know she was ill and distressed. I gave her what I hoped was a greeting of comfort. Not saying too much, I patted her reassuringly. I was quite anxious to do what I had come to do. I asked Norma to follow me into Lucille's family room. There would be time to visit later.

"Norma," I began, "I would like you to tell me about your mother's death, how she died, how you felt then and how you feel now."

"Finally, I placed the flowers at the front door and Bruce and I left. It wasn't unusual for her to be home and not answer her door or phone. She was known to just take off for God knows where and would only say that she had been away when asked about her whereabouts.

"There were signs that she had not been home recently. Flyers were strewn on the porch, there was mail in the box and a prescription had been left as well. Mother had an automatic delivery service for one of her medications. It was delivered by her local pharmacy on the same date each month.

"We left, went to church services, and returned later in the day. Again, no answer to our knocks. We rapped on several windows as well as the door. Finally, we decided to go home and try to reach her by phone. Our efforts were fruitless.

"I called a relative that evening on a chance he may know something we didn't but he hadn't heard from her in ages. I decided to wait for a few days. If I wasn't able to contact her by then, I would call the police.

"I was concerned about being taken seriously, my mother's habits being what they were. By Friday, I couldn't deal with the foreboding feelings any longer. From the first day I had this feeling in the pit of my stomach and it wouldn't go away. Bruce and I went to her house mid afternoon on Friday.

"I felt nauseous all the way there, my palms were sweaty and sweat ran down my face, my arms, my whole body. I asked Bruce what was that all around the front door as we pulled up to Mother's house.

"'I don't know, but look, it's all over the front window frames too,' Bruce said.

"We walked towards the front porch and I couldn't believe my eyes. 'My God in Heaven, maggots,' I screamed. Bruce took my arm, trying to steer me back to the car, but I wouldn't budge.

"'She's dead, my mother's dead in that house, and the maggots are crawling over her body,' I screamed.

"'I'm breaking in Norma,' Bruce warned, 'Stand back.'

"He broke a window and was driven back by the stench. 'I have to call the police, please wait in the car for me.' I was paralyzed, unable to move. Realizing I was in shock, Bruce helped me to the car. He returned after making the call, helped me from the car and together we walked around the house.

"Maggots were crawling out of every opening. There had to be thousands of them, and the stench surrounding the house was making me violently ill. Why hadn't someone called the police—all the mail and flyers were uncollected. Surely it must have struck someone as being odd. And those maggots and the smell. 'Why didn't we break in a week ago Bruce,' I sobbed.

"He held me, trying to comfort me, but I was inconsolable. She was my mother, even if she didn't love or want me, she was my mother. I should have done something sooner.

"When the police arrived, they only had to see the vermin crawling out of the house and smell the awful stench to know a dead person was inside. They radioed for an ambulance immediately.

"It's been almost a year since her death and the nightmare just keeps going on. I wasn't allowed in the house until it had been fumigated and cleared of all vermin. The carpet had to be lifted and when the health officials saw maggots underneath, they ordered the hardwood floors ripped up as well. Disinfecting and cleaning the house while waiting for health inspectors to examine the premises took a good deal of time, two months in fact. That's how long I had to wait to get into the house to clear out the contents.

"Mother tormented me in life and she continued after her death. Her hoarding habits shocked even me. I mean literally shocked me. When I was finally able to get up into the attic, I found piles and piles of old newspapers. Right to the ceiling. I found a few old trunks and went through them. In one, I found an urn. I opened it and couldn't believe my eyes. Ashes and bits of vertebrae is what I found.

"The bottom of the urn had the name and date of her first husband's death inscribed on it. She had been keeping this for fifty some years. Bruce and I had his remains interned in the cemetery as soon as we could, close to Mother. It seemed the proper thing to do.

"It took twelve dumpsters to clear out the junk from the house. We found government pension cheques totaling eighteen thousand dollars, outdated and no longer negotiable. The house was left to me and I was responsible for seeing that it was brought up to public health and city standards. Mother had left almost no money.

"We couldn't pay the estimated thirty-eight thousand dollars to bring the house up to city building codes. What a dilemma I was facing. Then I started getting sick, I don't mean just depression set in, I mean I was really sick.

Suddenly I developed a severe bladder illness. A foul smell exuded from my body. I developed high blood pressure, arthritis, and my feet became so painful I had to stay in bed for days at a time. I couldn't sleep, I roamed the house all night. I felt different. Mean and nasty. I didn't like anybody. I stopped caring about the children and Bruce. I stopped working and I would say things that didn't make sense. Bruce pointed out I was using words and phrases my mother had used in life. He told me one day I was just like my mother. He assured me it was not a compliment. I even had the same illnesses, he pointed out.

"But whatever I was doing or saying didn't bother me at all. It wasn't that I couldn't stop—I didn't want to stop. Then I saw Mother. She was standing at the foot of my bed. She had called my name and woken me at 3:15 a.m. 'I want you and your family to live in my house,' she said and then she just disappeared.

"I saw her several more times. Once I was on my way down to the laundry room when she materialized and pointed her finger at the pile of boxes that held her belongings. While I watched she moved, shrouded in ectoplasm, towards a box that she lifted up and carried upstairs. The closer she got to the doorway, the fainter her spirit became. There was a phone cord dangling from the box, and eventually all I could see was a box with a telephone cord heading up the basement stairs. It was left in the doorway.

"I wasn't frightened or surprised. I only knew that as soon as we could we would be moving into Mother's former house. This is what she wanted and I felt it was important to do. I didn't know why. She had indicated the same wish in the same way to my daughter Carol. Carol, going down the basement, was confronted by her grandmother's spirit. She was floating above the boxes and pointing to them and the stairs. 'Somehow, I just knew Gran was telling me to move her belongings back to the house, Mom.' Mother had formed a strange attachment to my daughter. When Carol was two years old, she tried to kidnap her from us.

"Bruce and I were on our way home from work when we passed Mother's car. It looked like she was moving, she did that a lot. It was Bruce who spotted Carol in the front seat. He turned the car around to follow them. He caught up, honked the horn and motioned for her to pull over, but she wouldn't. He sped ahead of her, cut her off and forced her to stop. Mother was furious. She hated Bruce, she cursed him, calling him every vile name she had in her colourful vocabulary.

"'What are you doing with Carol, I screamed at her?'

"'I'm taking her to Florida with me. I'm moving there.' Just like that, she was going to kidnap my daughter. She had come to our apartment and told the sitter she was taking Carol to a doctor's appointment. We spotted her when she was on her way out of the country.

"She refused to give Carol to us. Bruce and her had a fist fight. While they were doing that, the police arrived and I grabbed my daughter. The police asked if we wanted to press charges after hearing our story. We refused. But Mother pressed charges against Bruce for assaulting her. The case never was tried because Mother did move to Florida.

"She returned less than two years later. I knew she had a strange kind of love for Carol, so I allowed her to see our daughter when one of us was present. Soon after her return Mother was sent to prison for three years for defrauding a former employer. Carol barely remembered her or the kidnapping attempt when she was later released.

"She did keep her distance from her grandmother. Perhaps she sensed something unusual about her. I wasn't surprised that she appeared to Carol after her death. I believe that her mother cared for her, as much as she was capable.

"Since Carol is nineteen now I shared my experiences with her. I told her about the first time I saw Mother at the foot of my bed and her subsequent visits. I also explained the kidnapping incident to her and came clean about other startling events during Mother's lifetime.

"Carol is a second year psychology student at U. of T., it was she who explained to me what a psychopath is. The pain is so great, I want to die from it."

Her mother was doing her best to make it happen.

Tears continued to pour as she concluded her story. I had only spoken the word *theory* to Lucille, I gave no explanation. Only implying I had one. Now I had to disclose it to Norma.

"Norma," I began while handing her more kleenex, "I believe your mother's spirit is trying to possess you."

Her shoulders shook as she convulsed in sobs. "I believe you," she answered. "I've wondered myself about it."

"Your mother's entire motive throughout her life was to control. Since a person's personality accompanies them to the other side after death, your mother's objective is to never die and to continue her controlling. Her spirit has entered your body. This is why you feel so ill, old and tired. Right now your body is that of your eighty-four-year-old mother. This is why I wanted to meet you here today. I would like to end this possession."

"Please, Najla, do you think you could?" she asked.

"I know I can Norma, and I wanted to do it out of your home, because I believe it will be easier for your mother to depart from unfamiliar surroundings. I hope to confuse and weaken her, so that my mission will be less difficult to perform. This is why I asked you to meet me at Lucille's home, the home of someone we both know and trust. Lucille is totally unaware of my purpose in asking for this meeting. I wanted to speak with you, secure your permission for the exorcism."

"Lucille is my dearest friend, there's nothing she doesn't know about me, I wouldn't mind telling her anything, even something as terrible as this," Norma said.

"I realize that, but I can't intrude into your privacy, and make a disclosure of this nature to anyone other than you. I have gone against my own ethics in this case," I explained. "I never approach anyone with an offer of help. I must be asked. In view of our association however, I felt I could presume you would welcome my request," I offered.

"I'm so grateful you did, Najla, thank you for caring."

"Now, jut stretch out on the couch, relax and let me speak to your mother," I directed.

I walked over to stand above her, feeling curiously light as I did so. Normally a strong, heavy sensation runs through my body when I approach an exorcism. I knew at that point this would not be a difficult evacuation, so to speak. The room became unbearably cold, but once begun, I couldn't stop to fetch blankets for us. I had to continue!

I led Norma into a state of relaxation, explaining to her that I would count to ten, that I expected her to relax herself into a deep state of calm by the time I spoke the number ten. I slowly counted out the numbers one and two, I barely uttered three when Hilda spoke.

"I'm cold, I don't like being cold. Where am I? What am I doing here?"

"Where would you like to be Hilda?" I asked.

"Somewhere where it's warm, you know, like Florida."

"Were you ever in Florida, Hilda?"

"You know I was," she answered with a sharp snap in her voice. I noticed a marked change in her physical appearance. This is not unusual during a possession. The victim normally will have the mannerism and looks, as well as voice, of the deceased spirit. Now I was in the total and complete presence of Norma's dead mother, Hilda.

Since I never knew Hilda in life and I wanted some verification as to the authenticity of my subject, I planned on calling Lucille downstairs to witness the exorcism. But only after I felt absolutely certain I had the spirit under control. I had to be exact in my judgment, because if I wasn't Lucille would be the next victim of Hilda's possession.

Some spirits, in their exuberance to live, will latch on to an innocent bystander when confronted with exorcism. In other words, it becomes a random possession rather than a vendetta type of possession. I went on with my questions.

"How old are you Hilda?"

"Oh you know! I'm sixteen." She snapped this out.

"Where are you living?" She mentioned a town in Northern Ontario. "What are you doing with your life, are you happy?"

"Happy? How can I be happy for Christ sake, I'm pregnant." Venom poured from her.

"You're not looking forward to having a baby?"

"Jesus Christ! I'm pregnant with a married man's kid and you ask me if I'm happy!"

"All right, Hilda, let's move on now to after the baby's birth, she's a few months old, are you a happy mother?"

"I can't stand her, she cries all the time. Everybody condemns me for going out and having a good time. But I don't care, I go out anyway." The smug look on the face of the woman lying on the couch belonged to no one I knew, certainly not Norma.

Satisfied that this was a personal vendetta, I softly walked to the top of the basement stairs. Lucille was at the kitchen sink. I whispered her name. When she turned around, I put my finger to my lips, motioning for silence. I indicated I wanted her to follow me.

I observed Lucille as we approached Norma/Hilda. She looked totally stunned. I shook my head to indicate that she was to say nothing. I directed her to a chair and then walked over to my subject. I continued my line of questioning.

"Who takes care of your baby when you go out?"

"The landlady."

"Oh, you're not living at home?"

"You know they threw me out when they found out I was pregnant," she snapped. She assumed I knew because the subject experiences a feeling of familiarity with the person performing an exorcism. We connect somehow.

"Are you living alone?"

"Of course I'm living alone, who wants me, I have a baby. A brat, she's a brat," the resentful voice said.

"What did you name your baby?"

"Norma."

I looked over to where Lucille was sitting and saw tears flowing down her face. I walked over to her, put my hands on her shoulders and continued my line of questioning. I gently massaged Lucille's shoulders as I spoke with Hilda. What I intended doing was to relive Hilda's life with her by taking her back into the past and allowing her to release her venomous feelings towards her daughter.

Year by year I walked her through an unpleasant reverie. She disclosed a pattern of jealousy and resentment towards Norma, her children and her happiness with her husband Bruce.

"Hilda, Norma is two years old now, where are you living?"

"Alone."

"Where alone?"

"You know, Toronto."

"Where is Norma?"

"Where do you think, with my family."

"Why is she with your family?"

"They came with the Children's Aid people and took her away from me. They can have her too, see if I care. Now I'll enjoy my life."

"Do you ever have your daughter living with you again?"

"Yes," she said disgustingly, "They brought her back to me when I got married."

"Didn't you want her, Hilda?"

"Hell no, everybody fussing over her, saying how pretty she is, how smart she is, how good she is." She spoke these words in a taunting, childish manner.

I left Lucille's side to stand by Norma/Hilda. "Were you happy in your marriage, Hilda?"

"It was all right," she said indifferently. "He died."

"Who died?"

"My husband, who do you think?"

"What did you do with your life after he died?"

"Well, it wasn't easy, I had a little boy and that brat to take care of."

"How old was your son when your husband died?"

"Two."

"How did you take care or them?"

"I worked for a while as a waitress then I tended bar for a bit. Then I went to Florida."

"Was it very difficult for you to be on your own in Florida with two young children?"

"You know I didn't take the kids," she snapped.

"Where were the children?"

"Foster homes."

"It was fun, it was great."

"How long were you gone?"

"Till they found me."

"Who found you?"

"You know, the government people, the ones who sent me back."

"Were you happy to see your children again?"

"Didn't care."

"Who didn't care?

"For Christ sakes, I didn't care."

"When did your children live with you again?"

"When I married Nick."

"How old were they when you married him?"

"The kids, the kids, all you care about are the kids."

"How old were they when you married Nick."

"My son was eight and Norma was eleven."

"Did they live in foster homes for six years?"

"Yeah, so what? Wasn't I entitled to some freedom, to have a good time?"

"Did Nick like Norma?"

"He liked her too much, always fussing over her, spoiling her."

"Was it a happy marriage?"

"It was okay. He died."

"Who died?"

"Nick, Nick died."

"Were you a young widow?"

"I was thirty-three."

"How did the children react to Nick's death?"

"Sad. I yanked Norma out of school and put her to work," she said quite defiantly.

"Is this what she wanted?"

"Who cares, so what if she wanted to go to school. I had to work, and so did she. Brat, should have given her away when she was born. Did she stay with me, no, she got married. She should have been taking care of me, not a husband."

I glanced at Lucille who was now sitting on the edge of her chair, holding her hand over her mouth while non-stop tears flowed down her cheeks and onto her lap. I walked over, stood beside her and put my hand on her shoulder as I handed her a kleenex. I realized how very difficult this was for Lucille to witness.

"It's her mother," she whispered to me. "She even looks like her, that isn't Norma, it's Hilda."

"It's Hilda's voice," I said.

"Oh my God," Lucille whimpered.

I exerted pressure on Lucille's shoulders, intending to bring her out of her trauma. When I felt her relax a bit I went back to stand beside Norma/Hilda.

"Hilda, your children are grown now and you're living alone, what are you doing with your life?"

"Nothing, don't want to do anything. I want everybody to leave me alone. My son's dead, Norma's got that Bruce and her family, and I want them all to go away and leave me alone."

"Hilda, you're eighty-two years old now, you're living alone and you're very sick. Does anyone come to your home to care for you?"

"I told you I want to be left alone." She pounded her fists in the air as she said this.

"Hilda, how did you die?"

Her face contorted, and her hands flew first to her chest then her throat. "Hurts, it hurts," she gasped.

At this point it would have been possible for Norma to die because Hilda was in fact reliving her own death—being in Norma's body, death could have occurred again.

I had to move quickly and cautiously. "Hilda, listen to me. Let go, let go, you are not dying. You are dead, quickly now, tell me what you see. You are on the other side now, how do you feel?"

A confused look crossed over her face that was replaced by a calm, gentle demeanor. Her body relaxed and her hands went to her side.

"Warm, I'm so nice and warm. And it's so bright over here. There is a beautiful bright white light all around. It's so wonderful, I feel so peaceful here. I want to stay here. I don't ever want to leave."

"Hilda it's okay for you to stay there. This is where you are meant to be." Satisfied that Hilda was safely on the other side I now turned my attention to Norma and addressed myself to her.

"Norma, please relax, you are still in your state of meditation," I began. Very slowly she began to shift herself. "It's all right, Norma, everything is fine now, your mother has gone to her rest. It's safe for you to come back now."

A tremendous shudder ran through her body. She blinked her eyes rapidly. Several seconds passed before she recognized me. "What happened, I feel so strange," Norma said.

"Lucille would you please get a warm blanket for Norma." Lucille quickly dashed to comply. I sat on the sofa with Norma and put my arm around her. She felt like a block of ice and shivered uncontrollably. Lucille arrived with an afghan which we quickly wrapped around Norma. I stood to let Lucille sit by her friend. Norma would need her comfort now.

"Norma I'm going to go upstairs and warm up." I too was shivering with cold.

"I successfully put your mother to rest. You have no fear of further possession or apparitions. I'll leave Lucille here with you to tell you what happened during the exorcism. She's a perfect witness because she knew your mother during her lifetime. She can testify to you that your mother was indeed in your body."

I ran upstairs in need of two things, warmth and food. I was ravenously hungry and ate from the lunch table Lucille had prepared. I drank a hot cup of tea while wearing my winter coat. I had time to unwind sufficiently before Norma and Lucille joined me in the kitchen. Norma looked fresh and relaxed but Lucille was simply beside herself.

"Najla, how could her mother do that to her? It's horrible, just horrible," she said.

"Yes it was Lucille, but it's over now and life goes on," I said. I asked Norma how she felt.

"I feel good. Lucille told me everything—that I was possessed. She told me I looked and sounded like my mother, is that possible?"

"Not only is it possible, it's necessary for a spirit to manifest in that manner. I must have the total entity before me in order to deal with it. She had to come forward and show herself to me," I explained.

A very indignant Lucille spoke up. "That was Hilda— I knew her and I am certain that was her." It was very touching to see the closeness these two friends shared.

"I nearly didn't come today, Najla."

"Norma, I know that. It was your mother trying to stop you."

"I only have one question to ask. Is it right for me to move into my mother's house? Does she want me there?"

"Yes to both questions," I said. "You feel compelled to live in her former home because it's what she wants for you. Even psychopaths have some good in them," I explained. "I feel your mother is trying to make up for all she didn't do for you during her lifetime. In a way she will be 'taking care' of you from the other side. She will at last provide you with a home," I explained.

"Isn't that funny, Najla, that's what I thought."

"You'll feel physically stronger now. When your mother left her illnesses went with her."

We three sat around the kitchen table rehashing the morning's events till Norma said she had to get back home. When we were by ourselves I asked questions about Norma's life. It was important to have all the events that Hilda/ Norma described corroborated.

"By the way, how's your back and shoulder," I asked. A puzzled looking Lucille answered, "Gone, it's gone. What did you do?"

"A first for me," I answered. "An exorcism and a healing. When I placed my hands on you, while directing my questions to Hilda/Norma, I was concentrating on a healing for you."

"I don't believe it," Lucille said. "What a day this has been," Lucille said.

"How about you, Najla? Are you okay? Can I get you anything?"

"Some more hot tea and food," I answered.

The ending of this story is as I expected. Norma's physician visited her place of business two weeks after the exorcism. She expressed amazement at how well Norma looked. The doctor said to her, "You're glowing, you look healthy and vibrant. I'm amazed. Have you been healed?"

"Yes, I think I can say that I've been healed," was Norma's honest reply.